Advance Praise for
Awakening Healing Axis

"This work on self-compassion and self-understanding that Franny, Tim and the AHA team present sparked an awareness for me that changed the way I view myself. It gave me information that helped me understand my personal styles and expressions with respect to relationship dynamics and the tools with which to be compassionate and understanding with myself and others. The healing frequencies of Love encompass all of this information and for me provided the basis of a new way of looking at myself and the world." –Diane C.

"This guidebook to growth and self-love by Awakening Healing Axis lays out a sophisticated energetic map while simultaneously providing extremely practical everyday applications and approaches. For the majority of my life, I've been what I consider to be an energetically empathic and 'porous' person who's had difficulty grounding myself and setting energetic boundaries. Having taken the workshop where the authors brought forward the tools and information provided in this book, it has helped me to connect to Source and the essence of who I am. To feel and be more grounded and at home in my body and in general, and to recognize when I'm taking on energetic challenges that actually aren't mine to carry. It's also helped me start to develop tools to use when I find myself reeling, disconnected, or empathically bombarded. This information is a treasure for anyone who's energetically sensitive, who wants to feel more spiritually connected, or who cares about Planet Earth." –Bernadette H.

"Taking part in workshops and retreats with Awakening Healing Axis has benefited me personally and professionally. I truly feel the knowledge and innate knowing that I've gained from these experiences has allowed me to meet my most authentic self and *be present with others in a much more meaningful way. Franny and Tim make the path of learning energy healing a beautiful, fun, and heart-opening experience."* –Sylvie C.

"On the way to my first AHA retreat, a veteran of the prior retreats described them as 'life changing.' That they have been. It takes my energy work of 20 years to a new level, literally to a higher frequency for myself and for my clients. The material is presented in a 'retreat/ workshop' format: the 'retreat' for self-care, self-growth, and healing; the 'workshop' for understanding the material and learning treatment protocols to use in our work with our clients. Franny and Tim provide a nurturing and safe atmosphere interjected with lots of humor for both the instruction and experiential portions of the retreat. Over the years, I've learned that the focus of the specific topics is not as important as just being present with Spirit, with these gifted teachers, and with the fellow students. Participating with Awakening Healing Axis in their mission of 'aiding in the ascension of human conscious-ness aligned with the highest Rays of Divine Love' to help the planet and all of humanity has been a gift for me. As healers we are blessed with a calling to keep expanding in our work. AHA definitely provides these opportunities through the retreats, books, and online courses." –Billie S.

"Great retreat! So insightful! This is work that anyone can use. Not just healers. It should be a master class! I enjoyed the role playing and exercises as they brought clarity to the work. I feel I have documentation to help me recognize my expressions and help correct behaviors that don't benefit me today." –Melinda K.

Revealing
HIGHER FREQUENCIES

Awakening
Healing
Axis

Awakening Healing Axis Presents
Co-Authors Franny Harcey & Tim McConville
Foreword by Catherine Morgan

INSPIREBYTES OMNI MEDIA

Revealing Higher Frequencies
A Guidebook to Exploring Personal Growth and Self-Love Through Deep Reflection Using the Divinity Mirror and Energetic Expressions

Distributed globally with Expanded Distribution by KDP.

ISBN Paperback: 978-1-953445-49-0
ISBN E-Book: 978-1-953445-50-6
Library of Congress Control Number: 2023952365

 INSPIREBYTES OMNI MEDIA

Inspirebytes Omni Media LLC
PO Box 988
Wilmette, IL 60091
For more information, please visit www.inspirebytes.com.

AHA Statement

"Our mission is to raise the collective frequency of ourselves and those we support, so that we can aid in the ascension of human consciousness aligned with the highest Rays of Divine Love."

Table of Contents

Foreword

By Catherine Morgan

Love moves all things forward, and so it is with this book, the third in Awakening Healing Axis' commitment to sharing their groundbreaking work in elevating human consciousness through the energy field. This time, this group of dedicated healers in physical and Spirit form have focused their light on bringing forth ways to nourish the self through powerful yet accessible methods. This book offers a great opportunity to explore, reflect, and expand on the personal journey of growing our soul towards embodying more light and more love.

As a longtime student of AHA's work, I can say it has created shifts for me in ways that no other practice has. In addition to the innovative protocols, what has impressed me the most over the years is AHA leaders Franny and Tim's commitment to walking their talk, embodying what they teach, staying in integrity, and supporting their students every step of the way. They have gone above and beyond in answering Spirit's call, and Spirit has responded in a big way. AHA holds a matrix of spiritual helpers and teachers on all levels that have stepped forth to make this great work happen. And in this book, you have a chance to build your own powerful connections with this group for your personal healing and expansion.

One of Tim and Franny's gifts is that they have the ability to bring down elevated concepts and make them relatable in step-by-step methods that are easily applied. In these pages, I was grateful to experience their powerful invocations and affirmations that created immediate shifts with reminders of who I am as a being. I also explored practices allowing me to reflect on how I walk in the world and what the world mirrors back to me, bringing me more consciousness of the choices I make.

It was also a great opportunity to deepen my understanding of AHA's foundational work in practices to shift my energy to higher frequencies. From that place, the outlined work of clearing the energy field—from soul contracts to trauma energy to labels and misconceptions—becomes that much more powerful. The book also seeks to step beyond what needs to be healed to help identify and celebrate the unique spiritual gifts each of us brings to the planet. And, in these times of unprecedented change, I appreciated the opportunity the book brings to align with the larger, higher frequencies affecting us all.

Ultimately, AHA has always remembered that this great body of energetic work must first and foremost be embodied at the human level, and in this book, AHA returns to the core of what humans are here to learn— how to love. For in Love, the human remembers the Divine.

Think of this book as a gallery filled with richly colored paintings. Each section is like a painting, a beautiful landscape to step into and explore, to contemplate and enjoy. It isn't a book to be rushed through. It is a book to be savored. I recommend letting it work through you slowly, letting it percolate. Just reading the words will start an energetic elevation. You may choose to start at the beginning and read through, or let the section you need call to you. I tell you it also makes great bedtime reading and a great way to start your day. It is written in such a way that you can explore its teachings in your time, taking what is valuable to you at any given moment.

Finally, I would say this book opens the way to embodying more of who you are. Think of a door opened a crack, letting in just a sliver of light. Then imagine being able to swing open that door fully so the light can stream through. This is what AHA's work enables you to do.

Oh, what a joy.

Wishing you the best on your journey of discovery,
Catherine Morgan, *Author, Healer, and Energy Fields Enthusiast*
Summer 2023

Part 1

Fundamental Principles

Chapter One

Introduction

This third book builds on the foundation provided by the first two books, *Awakening to Higher Frequencies* and *Embodying Higher Frequencies: Accelerating Personal and Planetary Consciousness.* This is part of a continually expanding series that brings forth higher frequency work. Our first books covered the work in 2020 and 2021. The work presented here represents Awakening Healing Axis' (AHA) thoughts following our Spring 2022 workshop/retreat, ninth in our ever-evolving body of work. Each workshop focuses on a new topic and contains mostly new material. This workshop's focus was self-understanding, self-love, self-compassion, and healthy personal energetic boundaries. Spirit has nudged us to disseminate this work of raising our energetic frequency in print form with associated web-based visual teachings.

For those who have read the previous volumes, much of the background material will seem familiar. We have made some updates to the high frequency shift process as well as refinements to the descriptions of the energetic world we perceive. Enough has changed that we recommend reviewing these sections, even if you have read our material previously. The guidebook portion describing experiential protocols for self and client is all new material for your exploration.

Our early work was developed with the original triad of healers. As this work unfolds, we are urged to expand our contributors and facilitators. This volume includes work developed by our emerging team of associates.

We focus here on self-development and understanding how the mirrors and filters of our beliefs and energetic coping mechanisms distort our worldview and interactions with others. We begin with focusing on self-love, as it seems to be at the root of our interactions with the world. We believe that we are here in "earth school" to learn lessons. All those lessons have something to do with love. Our ability to understand love is constrained by our ability to self-love. We also focus deeper into personal energetic boundaries and how we regulate those boundaries to interact with the energies of those around us. This self-discovery is a key aspect of learning to be more present and hold higher frequencies.

In order for humanity as a whole to awaken, we must each awaken as individuals. We are all connected on this planet, so our individual awakening contributes to the collective awakening. We are in a distinct time period for all of humanity to awaken and embrace our rapid evolution into a new energetic world. Rather than wait for the collective awakening to sweep us along, we invite you to be explorers at the forefront of this wave. This work provides essential tools for the self-transformation needed to sustain the energetic expressions of this evolutionary step. When we take those steps to move ourselves to a higher frequency, we can then become the conduit for healing the planet and lifting all others.

As long-time energy workers and instructors, AHA began as a triad; we joined each other to create a shift in ourselves and, in turn, those we train. We are often asked what difference it makes if we raise our frequency or vibration. Let us start with clearing up a little language about vibration.

The New Age movement commonly uses the phrase "raising vibration." However, vibration is movement, and frequency is the rate of that movement. We are actually always vibrating, so we do not really "raise" the vibration. We raise the frequency or rate of the vibration.

Compare it to sound. Increasing vibration (volume) just makes things louder. Raising the frequency (pitch) of sound, however, moves it to a higher note. So we need to focus on frequency and move our energy to a higher note.

If we think about frequency within the context of our emotions and thoughts, lower frequencies are associated with more difficult and less joyful states such as anger, frustration, fear, and negativity. Higher frequency emotions are associated with more positive expressions such as love, joy, hope, and awe.

Spiritually, we are designed to constantly strive for closer connections to the Divine and experience deeper love. This too requires a higher frequency. Therefore, raising your frequency allows for greater happiness and more cohesive interpersonal relationships.

Additionally, many illnesses have psychosomatic components that have been linked to stress and long-term existence in states of lower frequency. This has been particularly noticeable in the realms of autoimmune disorders. Raising our frequency helps move us into a place of less disease and more efficient bodily function. The benefits of holding a higher frequency show up in a multitude of forms throughout our lives such as: improved health, deeper alignment with goals, more positive relationships, more stable and uplifted mental health, and a richer spiritual life.

We think it is important to have a daily practice of intentionally raising our frequency. Additionally, being mindful of frequency as we interact with others and the world throughout our day is also essential. Most of us cannot hold these higher frequencies without making a conscious effort to nudge it back up as it drifts down.

Higher frequency work is continuing to change those of us who facilitate Awakening Healing Axis in subtle ways. As we are better able to sustain higher frequency, it changes the way we work with clients, teach energy work classes, and interact with people in our lives. We have noticed that although we teach the exact same curriculum as our old classes, the students seem to be getting more out of them, and the work runs deeper. The collective continues to grow as we continue to facilitate, and those who have shared in workshops expand in awareness and are clearly all connected in this work. Spiritually, we sense that we are able to connect at a deeper level and receive greater guidance as our world has become much richer and more expansive. We are still quite capable of experiencing a lower frequency, but we find that we spend less time there and can pull ourselves up more easily.

Though easy to learn, the capacity to shift frequency requires continued practice. It has the potential to change each of us in amazing ways, and the ripples can change our entire planet. We believe frequency shift is one of the keys to human and planetary evolution.

Importance of Science

We strive to respect what we know in terms of current science, especially when we expand beyond the known limitations of our current understanding. Tim is trained in scientific methods and is keenly interested in the scientific understanding of our wonderful world. When referring to scientific principles, we do our best to be accurate within our understanding.

It is also important to realize the nature of scientific study. As a society, we are continually learning new things about our world. If we stop to think about it, we realize that almost all science texts from our college days are virtually useless due to the expansion in knowledge. One generation from now, scientific understanding will have again exponentially increased. How can we possibly state that we completely understand our world when every day there is a new scientific discovery in areas we thought we understood?

We need to respect scientific understandings yet not let them limit us from exploring beyond those confines. Any good physicist will agree that there are many more dimensions than the 3D view suggests. Various theories predict from 11 to 30 dimensions or more, yet we know almost nothing about these spaces. As such, it is important for us to both include science in the conversation and remain open to its ever-evolving nature and our understanding of the world.

How to Use This Work

This work is laid out as a guidebook. That means we will describe how we work and our perspective on the energetic world. Additionally, we offer you guided protocols to use these concepts. The protocols can be used on oneself to aid in healing and personal transformation. They can also be used by an experienced energy therapist to work with clients. We consider this to be advanced work that adds to the skillset of practitioners trained in one or more healing modalities.

When we facilitate this work in workshops, we find the work is repeatable. Our theory is that in the workshop setting, the facilitators model the energetic frequency of the Guides and the work. Through the entrainment process, the energy systems of the participant resonate with the frequencies of the facilitator(s). The participant is then able to reproduce those frequencies once exposed. It does not require conscious awareness or understanding on the part of the participant. Their energy system does what is required on an unconscious level.

Of course, we realize that not everybody will have the time, money, and flexibility required to physically attend one of our workshops in person. Additionally, we had previously been a little dubious that the subtle frequencies that define the depth of this work can be fully translated via web-based teaching. However, we have found that recorded audios and video serve a respectable role in transmitting and entraining these frequencies.

With this in mind, we will be creating a web-based series of teaching to accompany this book. It is our sincere hope that the combination of printed material and web-based video content will provide the proper combination of material that satisfies both the mind's need for information and the heart's need for energetic connections. We have seen immense transformations in our workshop participants. Our hope is that broader availability of the material can aid many more people in their healing and make a positive impact on humanity.

Chapter Two

Importance of Higher Frequencies

As energy therapy and healing practitioners, we are often confronted with situations of chaos and fear. Some are more extreme than others, but nevertheless they all tug at our own insecurities and may trigger trauma and/or unresolved personal issues. The question then becomes, "How do we stay afloat in these stormy seas of energies and provide a safe refuge for ourselves and others?" On the surface, it would seem as if our daily self-care, peaceful life choices, and healing work are enough to fend off the destructive forces of judgment, prejudice, hatred, fear, shame, guilt, or arrogance. This is not an easy nor simple task, especially when we are confronted by unexpected and/or extreme situations.

The ability to shift our frequency is something everyone can learn, but it requires continued practice and attention. Personal commitment to this choice can shift each of us in amazing ways. One of the first tools for manifesting such a shift is discernment. There are many "channels" of energy, or energetic radio stations, in the energy realms. We are bombarded in our daily interactions with numerous aspects of the lower frequency channels, many of which are reinforced by social media, marketing, and many of the news headlines. The much more desirable higher frequency channels, such as "selfless love" and "random acts of kindness," are not publicized as often nor made popular by the media. Thus, it becomes very important to proactively tune in to the bigger picture of what is really happening. Good discernment involves asking if this situation or information is of the light, and whether it should be accepted or ignored. One of the easiest ways to be proactive in our discernment is to tune in to nature.

In the natural world, spring is a time of new energies and perhaps the easiest time to see new beauty in nature. We can always be nourished by what nature offers to help keep us grounded and whole. Choosing to tune in to nature and a more positive worldview changes our overall perceptions and raises our frequency. Take the time to drink in the mystery of nature's beauty and the inherent goodness of humanity. Awe and wonder can shift our body, emotions, mind, and Spirit to states of bliss and joy, giving us a glimpse of the altered states of the mystics and prophets. Choose compassion and take the "high road" as much as possible.

Unfortunately, mass media seems to choose the extremes, demonizing or falsely elevating people. Everyone is a mix of both good and bad. No one is without flaws. All we can hope for is to act like our better selves most of the time. We are all in this together, and the more we support one another and work as a synergistic team, the more we will be able to fuel hope and help maintain our individual and collective equilibrium. In this manner, each of us can hold space for the ongoing evolution and ascension of humanity and our planet.

In our collective work, we focus on strengthening and broadening the deepest cores of our human and spiritual existence. This involves high frequency techniques and protocols for transmuting and elevating our abilities to be fully present in this realm, all the while anchored into the core of our earth. This empowers us to stand as conduits for Divine energies of unconditional love—and by fully embodying our Divine light as human and Spirit, we have the ability to step into a space of healing at a quantum level. From this place, we can help raise the frequency of our clients and others around us to support the healing and enlightenment of all.

Chapter Three

How We Work

Our original triad was drawn together in the process of various activities in the Healing Touch Program (HTP) organization. The founder of the Healing Touch Program, Janet Mentgen, also serves as a Guide to our work as Awakening Healing Axis (AHA). When instructing previous HTP classes, we often felt Janet's presence in the classroom although Janet had left the earth plane. We also sense her presence and guidance in this more advanced work. As presenters and active members in national and international-level organizational activities, we would frequently connect with each other and compare notes about our expanding energetic interests. We found that we were each getting nudged by Spirit to expand the work beyond the envelope of current HTP teachings.

Sometime around 2016, we decided to work together to create an advanced workshop. As the planning unfolded, we realized that this was bigger than one workshop. Led by Spirit, we all said "Yes!" and we committed to the unknown by formalizing a business partnership to move the work forward. We have found the idea of working as a triad to be quite valuable. Discernment is critical in guided or channeled work. The triad organizational model provided the necessary validation checks for each other and allowed expanded creativity. Often one of us gets a part of the information, and the others build on it and expand to find what was missing. The old saying "two minds are better than one" seems enhanced by adding a third.

We continue to work in triads or larger groups as we believe it is important to get clarification and validation of guided input. Input from the guides can come in the quiet times of meditation for any of the group or perhaps as we ponder the work, or when writing. Often when we are collaborating with clients, we get guidance to shift the energy in new and unusual ways. During our times together, we may collectively hone the work brought in by one of us, or we may bring in innovative ideas on potential energetic topics. All the creative ideas and techniques are tested with willing clients and refined prior to bringing the healing work forward in a workshop. Often, information comes in swiftly and takes time to unpack and re-package in a suitable workshop format. A 20-minute burst of the latest information can take months to translate into teachable workshop segments. Part of that translation process is to find appropriate real-world analogs that can help bridge the understanding.

We believe that it is important that this more esoteric work weaves with current scientific understanding of our world and the physical body where possible. This allows us to understand how energetic work complements medical interventions within the limitations of ever-expanding scientific knowledge.

Chapter Four

Energetic Framework

To really access the work in this book, it is important to first understand our viewpoint of the unseen aspects of the human energetic system. This understanding both informs the work and assists in directing the intent of our protocols.

We believe our existence on this planet is far more complex than the physical and mental framework often portrayed by scientific understanding. Our existence and interactions with others is a multidimensional experience. The understanding we offer builds upon the teachings of other mystics and explorers of this area. Over time, our guides have continued to expand our understanding of this framework. If you have studied this subject widely enough, you are aware that there are inconsistencies in terminology and differing explanations.

We liken this phenomenon to the old story of a group of blind men describing an elephant as they touch distinct parts. Each may be correct yet provide only a partial view of the whole.

Just like the blind men in the story, we are limited in the ways we experience the world beyond our five senses. Each of us—each energetic explorer—has different gifts to experience the unseen. All may be correct, but all are still limited by the gifts of the seer. So what happens when we are faced with the significant issue of our human desire to linearize and fit the multidimensional universe into a 3D box? It simply does not work. It would be akin to making two-dimensional drawings of ten-dimensional objects just so they fit in a book.

Therefore, the following is our attempt to describe our current and ever-evolving understanding of our energetic framework. In offering this information, we acknowledge that our limited human minds are only marginally capable of accurately understanding and translating the infinite into the finite. Again, like the blind men, we can report what we see with accuracy, but the true scope of the whole still resides in the mist.

We think of ourselves in this human existence as a bridge between heaven and earth. We are very much a Spirit and part of all that exists in the realm of Spirit. Our lessons are solidly placed in this school on the planet earth. Our description of our energetic framework begins with the earth that we are connected to, then moves back to our origin, which is in the realm of Spirit in order to describe how we transcend both of these realms.

Grounding

Being grounded in this earthly existence is probably one of the most important—yet least practiced—spiritual disciplines. Although there are many techniques and plenty of teachers with the message, there seem to be few people who put it to practice. The combination of 1) a western culture that overvalues the mental, and 2) spiritual guidance that shames the physical and directs our gaze upward has created a culture of people living in the upper Chakras.

We passionately believe that we are all at the juncture of heaven and earth. We have a choice to be that bridge between the two, or the gap between the two. For many workshop participants, it seems counterintuitive that to raise our frequency high, we must first connect deeply below. We have seen many times when working with participants that the key to accessing the energy of above is to first look below. We suggest that an important part of any healing work discipline is to start with the awareness of being grounded and consciously connected to the earth.

The hard part is to then maintain that connection and stay grounded while experiencing lofty higher frequencies and multiple dimensions. One of the keys to achieving this is practice. With practice, we can spread the awareness of being grounded and in the present moment to our everyday life. We aren't suggesting that it is likely we will stay grounded at every waking moment. Slowly gaining a larger percentage of our day would be an achievable goal.

While being grounded is important in spiritual work, it does have benefits in our everyday activities. When we are grounded, we tend to be more aware of our surroundings. We are more able to see the beauty of nature and the people around us. When grounded, we are also less scattered and more present. Our personal interactions and conversations are far richer when we are grounded and paying attention to others. A great many of those moments of forgetfulness or absent-minded mistakes come from being ungrounded. When we forget where we misplaced something, we probably put it down while our mind was in the past or future and we were ungrounded. Grounding is an aspect of being present, of living in the now.

Pure Timeless Earth Template

As noted above, we are big proponents of connecting or "grounding" to the earth. In our practice, we have noticed that many people, especially the more sensitive people, have trouble connecting to our planet. Some people more naturally "ground" into other elements than earth. Some prefer water, air, wood, ether, or some other substances. Many of the sensitive people find the earth feels unsafe to them, which makes it difficult to ground into the earth—or stay grounded if they can connect to it. We have been striving to find a way for these people to feel safe enough to make a deeper connection to the planet, which we share in more detail below through the concept of Gaia.

Another issue that is occurring is the ascension movement. Numerous groups and individuals around the planet are participating in efforts to shift the energetic frequency of the planet, moving earth and its inhabitants into a higher frequency or dimension. Most of these efforts are good; however, there is some distortion. It seems to us that although the effort is good, there is a lack of cohesion, and divergent groups have slightly different ideas about the frequency and direction in which we are headed. We liken the situation to an orchestra warming up with instruments out of tune. We are lacking a common note to harmonize with that will allow us to come into perfect cohesion.

Our suggested solution to these issues is termed "Pure Timeless Earth Template." Rather than tuning into the current earth, or the idea of an evolving earth, we offer the idea of a Divine template of a pure projection of perfect earth in resonance with the organizing principles of the universe. Another way to think of this is to use the idea of Gaia. This idea has the earth as a manifestation of a Divine being. If we think of Gaia, we will ground into the pure, Divine aspects of the earth. When offered a model of connecting to the Divine aspect of the earth, or the Pure Timeless Earth Template, most people can more readily ground and feel safer connecting to the frequency of earth. The Pure Timeless Earth Template offers a consistent, safe frequency that all of us can use to come into harmony and resonance.

We have adopted the Pure Timeless Earth Template in all of our grounding exercises. Our Hara, grounding, and Vivaxis connecting exercises all now use this frequency to hold connection to our planet. We have found that this provides a stronger and more pure connection. We are noticing a deeper degree of connection to the planet, the ability to hold the connection longer, and greater ease of coming into resonance with the matrix of the earth. Many who were once hesitant to energetically connect with our earth can now embrace her at this new frequency.

Core Essence

We think of Core Essence as our true self—the fundamental, multidimensional, spiritual being that we are. This is the purest aspect of who we are and is in resonance with the oneness of everything. At this level, we are pure and untainted by the trials and tribulations of living on earth. This aspect of our being is not harmed and never traumatized. Core Essence exists in a different dimension. This highest frequency of our spiritual being cannot be fully experienced on the physical plane. Just as electricity is stepped down from high voltage lines by transformers to household current levels, our Core Essence gets stepped down into the lower frequencies of our existence to manifest on the physical plane.

We consider soul to be a subset of Core Essence. Soul holds more earthbound characteristics. Perhaps soul is more like the level of consciousness needed to bridge the dimensional realities and manage our lessons while on the earth plane. Our concept of Core Essence is like what Barbara Brennan described in her book, *Light Emerging*, as

Core Star.[1] Her visuals of Core Star show it as located in the middle of the body, just above the navel. That may have been generally true in 1993 when her work was published, but we now visualize that it normally expresses itself at a higher location in the body and is more adaptable to movement. Core Essence exists in another dimension, so it is not actually present in the physical body as tissue. Visually identifying these aspects within our physical self is a useful tool that helps our limited minds work with these concepts.

Keep in mind that Core Essence (or Core Star) is a higher dimension of self and not really located within the physical realm, yet it can be perceived to be located somewhere along the centerline of the body. As we mature spiritually, it can be perceived as moving higher in the physical body. In fact, humanity's collective evolution is allowing Core Essence to move higher and higher. Our concept of Core Essence allows greater fluidity and movement with an individual's frequency. Our work encourages that elevation, with the goal of raising the perceived location out of the space of physical manifestation and into the spiritual energetic layers.

We sense Core Essence to be quite a malleable part of our energy self. It can be expanded, contracted, and elevated as one learns to master and better regulate the expression of their energetic being.

The Hara

Our understanding of the Hara is rooted in the work of Barbara Brennan. We believe that channeled work from the 1990s is a solid foundation. However, we are constantly evolving in an energetic sense. Therefore, it is best to see the earlier work as a good introduction, realizing that we may now be different in subtle and important ways. The Hara exists in the dimension of intention. Decades ago, Brennan's work suggested that it was the fourth dimension. Our guidance now tells us to simply say another dimension rather than labeling any specific dimension.

Defining the Hara requires an understanding of the concept that our intention to incarnate on planet earth manifests an energetic

---

1 Brennan, B. A. (1993). *Light Emerging; The Journey of Personal Healing.* Bantam Books.

connection between our Core Essence and the earth. That energetic connection is held in place by the intentionality of being incarnate and becomes the basis and foundation for our physical and energetic bodies. Although the Hara is probably a multidimensional holographic projection, Brennan's description is much easier to understand.

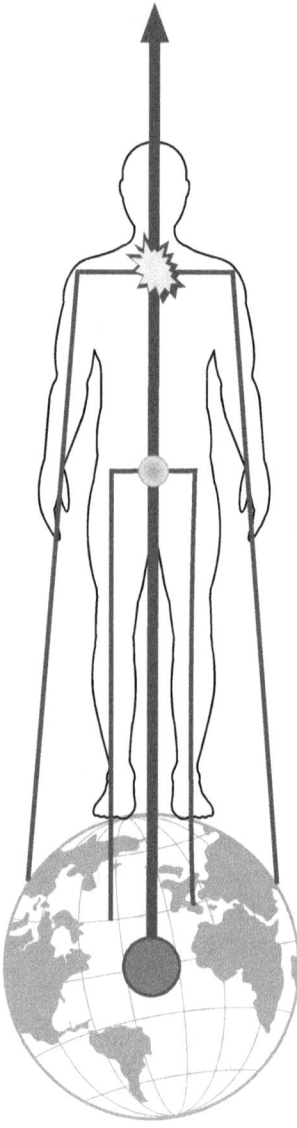

The Hara begins to take form with the intent to incarnate, which means it begins to manifest well before our birth. In our work, we have sensed an incoming child's energy system well before conception. The Hara, therefore, is a line of energy connected to the core of planet earth. Along that line of energy there are three aspects of the Hara: the Tan Tien, Soul Seat, and Point of Individuation (ID). The Tan Tien is in our lower abdomen. The Soul Seat is near the thymus gland, and the ID point is located at a point above our head where the aura starts. Keep in mind that the Hara is in another dimension, so it will not be physically found within the body.

The Hara becomes the foundation of our earthly energetic system. Brennan also describes the Hara as carrying a unique, specific sound note or frequency. That unique individual frequency is part of the definition of who we are on this planet. Our Chakras and fields then develop around the Hara. Each of the three aspects of the Hara have certain characteristics:

• The Tan Tien carries the note and makes the physical connection to the Hara. The Tan Tien is used extensively in martial arts training.

- The Soul Seat holds our spiritual longings and desires.
- The ID point holds our connection to Spirit or Divine energy.

As the Hara holds our intentionality to be on earth, it also contains a connection to our life's purpose. The stronger and more aligned one's Hara is, the better the realization and alignment to life's purpose. Subsequently, if one's intentionality to be on earth is not clear, it will energetically appear as some level of distortion in the Hara.

Brennan described the Hara as a laser line of light, and students carry forward that visual of a very thin Hara line. However, it is our experience that the Hara can be much wider. Perhaps it is due to evolutionary shifts in our energy structure over the last few decades. Our perspective is that a wider Hara can carry more energy. We often use the metaphor of a garden hose versus a fire hose. The larger hose allows for a much greater flow of water, so a larger Hara allows more energy flow. That said, we also caution that one needs to be able to regulate and control the amount of energy flow. Bigger is not necessarily better if you cannot properly use it.

We have been slowly increasing the size and expansion of the Hara that we teach in our work. One must slowly increase the size as they learn to regulate and control the extra energy. At a recent workshop, we had participants expand and experience an increasingly wider Hara with instructions to bring it back to what felt right after experiencing the expansion. There were several reports of people then having tripped circuits and other electrical issues with the technological devices in their lives. One even reported seeing a light that would not go out, unscrewing the bulb, and having the bulb still glowing in their hand. Although amusing, such dysregulation is not very practical for living in our normal 3D realities. We need to effectively manage these new, higher frequencies of being.

We also experience and bring forward the visualization that the Hara has four additional strengthening lines that are not separate from the Hara, but part of it. From the Tan Tien, lines extend to each hip and down each leg. From the Soul Seat, lines extend to each shoulder and down each arm. These additional pillars (as the previous graphic depicts) support additional grounding into the gridlines and matrices of the Pure Timeless Earth, inviting stronger connection to our planet.

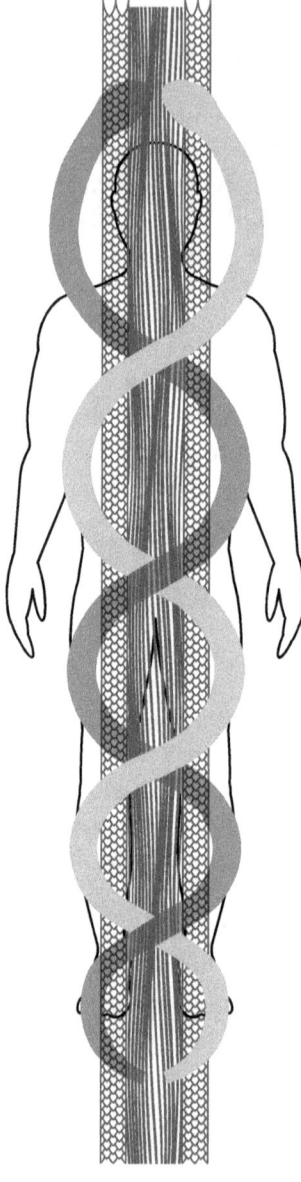

The Hara has structure, both internal and external. We sense the outside structure of the Hara as a woven expression with the weave expressions spiraling in both clockwise and counterclockwise directions. Similarly, there seem to be internal structures of opposite spirals, much the way Kundalini energy is often depicted.

The Hara can distort in a wide variety of ways. Distortion can be related to past life trauma or lack of clarity in the intentionality of incarnation. Traumas in this life can also impact the Hara, causing leaks, tears, or distortions. Distortions may cause it to tilt at an angle either above or below, limiting connections to either earth or Source energies. A healthy Hara should be straight, like a column of light. Leaks and tears in the Hara may limit access to full energy flow and ultimately can lead to disease or illness. The Hara can also become weak and poorly defined when intentionality to be on earth wanes. We have seen this at the end of life or even in children who are struggling with life on earth, having recently reincarnated.

The Hara, like all aspects of our energy structure, can be healed, upgraded, and repaired with the help of skilled energy workers. These helpers could be incarnate or in the spirit realm. Our work includes practices to repair and keep regular energetic hygiene of our Hara and also helps our clients do the same.

The Vivaxis

The Vivaxis and the Hara are completely different energetic structures and likely exist in different dimensions. Both are equally important but in quite diverse ways. The Hara begins sometime before conception or during our time in the womb, whereas the Vivaxis energetically makes a connection near the time of our birth. We choose to incarnate into a specific family in a certain physical location for our lessons in earth school. The Vivaxis is a specific connection to the earth that you anchor into at that location on the earth where you choose to incarnate.

We create a little energetic sphere that anchors in and to the earth and connects to us as we move around, like a virtual cord. It stays anchored there throughout your lifetime unless it is intentionally moved to a different location. This cord allows energy to flow, completing a circuit between the earth and ourselves. Our bones and fascia are the chief carriers of our Vivaxis forces. The Vivaxis is an anchoring force to the earth. When clear and flowing, the Vivaxis feeds us with minerals and nutrients from the earth. This flow is on a frequency level and does not actually transport minerals physically.

We sense this flow of energy via the Vivaxis coming into the body up the left leg. We sense it quite strongly, almost like a hose in the lower leg and bones. As it moves up the leg, it begins to disperse into the fascia tissues as well. It continues up the body, crossing the heart to the right side, then moves up around the head from right to left. It then flows back down, crossing the heart again, and exits the body along the entire right side. We find it more difficult to sense the return flow on the right as it is much more dispersed than the concentrated flow coming into the body.

We have also become aware that the Vivaxis is somehow energetically interwoven with the 10th Chakra. We do not sense that the Vivaxis flow is through the 10th Chakra, however. It seems that changes in the Vivaxis interact with and affect the 10th Chakra. That interaction could be in the quantum relationships of all aspects of our energy system.

The primary focus of our work is to help people reestablish and maintain healthy Vivaxis connections. Prior to joining together, we had dabbled with the concept of Vivaxis connections and were aware of the books on the subject. However, it was not until we were working together with AHA that we began to understand the importance of the Vivaxis. We recommend reading *The Vivaxis Connection* by Judy Jacka, ND, who had studied Fran Dixon's work. Again, we see this early work as a good foundation, although we have a somewhat different sense about certain aspects. Jacka goes into a great amount of detail about the chemical aspects of the Vivaxis, which we have not felt drawn to explore yet. We feel that this would be a great area of exploration for someone who focuses on energetic rather than product-based approaches to micronutrition.

Our healing work includes sensing and working with the Vivaxis. As healers, it is important that we do our self-care work and maintain a healthy Vivaxis. When assessing our own or a client's energy system, the Vivaxis is an important element to check. When working locally, we usually do this while standing at or holding the client's feet. When working remotely or for self, we just tune in to the flow of energy in the Vivaxis.

To do this, the first step is to feel into the Vivaxis flow at the left foot to assess the connection. Then focus on the energetic sphere where the Vivaxis connects to the earth. It is possible that the sphere is not functioning properly or is not integrated into the gridwork of the earth at that locality. Sometimes it appears the sphere is just dormant. When assessing and working with the sphere, again ask for help from Spirit. Visualize the sphere as radiant. Ask that the energetic structure of the sphere be upgraded and allow it to fuse and integrate with the highest frequencies of the local earth matrix.

For many people, the Vivaxis has just become sluggish and less effective, analogous to a pipe that has become clogged and corroded. For those cases, ask the spirit helpers to help shift the Vivaxis flow to its optimum function at this time. We often envision iridescent colors flowing into the Vivaxis as it is cleared and restructured.

Unfortunately, for some people, the Vivaxis does not even connect to the earth. We have seen a few individuals where the Vivaxis seems to float above the earth, not connecting to it, or even connecting to a portal or other dimensions. Sometimes trauma related to the original connection or a distortion of the earth at the original connection makes it difficult to reestablish a good connection. In some cases, it has been beneficial to move the Vivaxis connection to a more supportive location on earth. Moving the Vivaxis should not be taken lightly and should only be done with spiritual help and guidance. Additionally, moving it to a place based on ego-related whims may not be in the person's highest good. The work of Jacka and Dixon suggests that the movement of the Vivaxis needs to be done with a physical process. We believe it can be managed by the purest of intentions and projection of consciousness.

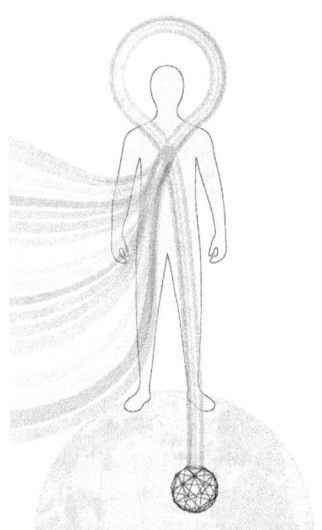

The Chakra System

The techniques and the energetic framework we are given include a considerable amount of work with the Chakra system. We initially focused primarily on the traditional seven Chakras, but also worked with some of the Chakras not contained in the body structure. There is a sizable amount of inconsistent information regarding Chakras in the world. A quick search of the internet yielded systems ranging from six to 114 different Chakras, and there are probably even more ideas out there. In general, our view of the Chakra system is similar to the 12-Chakra system described by author Cyndi Dale. We suggest referencing her material for a deeper explanation of the Chakras. Our explanations below will only provide enough information to locate the Chakras and work with them within the broader context of our higher frequency techniques.

Chakras are concentrated energy centers in and around our body. Chakras function as part of our sensory system and regulate energy flows to keep our body functioning at optimum levels. Although the term Chakra comes from the Sanskrit term for wheel or disk, we think the torus is a better explanation for the shape of a Chakra. The torus is a basic natural shape of energetic structures.

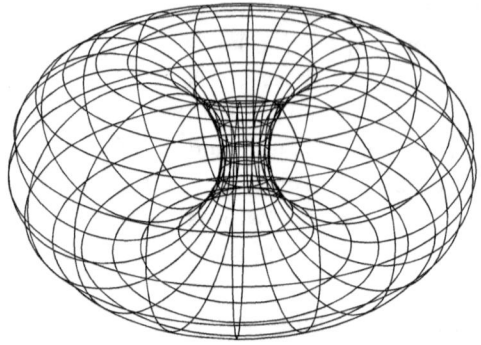

Examples of toroidal energy flow are exhibited throughout nature from the largest galactic structures to the tiniest biological functions and even smaller. This is the shape that concentrations of electromagnetic energy take. Viewing Chakras from this natural perspective also validates both of the common beliefs that Chakras look like disks and that they look like cones. It just depends on the viewer's perspective.

We think of the Chakras as having a front side, a back side, and a center point that connects front and back. The front aspect, which is governed by the physical laws, relates to the conscious self and our day-to-day realities. It holds and senses information about our current life, needs, decisions, and experiences. The front allows the tangible world to help us.

The back aspect, which is governed by limitless alternative realities, represents the unconscious self and information about our past. It holds imprints from our past lives, past experiences and decisions, and needs. The back allows the intangible world to help us.

The center point we sometimes refer to as the "zero point." The center point of the Chakra is located along the central channel of the energy system or Hara. The center point is the access point of pure potential or the zero point field. When the central point is activated, we can call in the next expression of our highest light. The zero point can seem to be formless; we often experience it as opening into a vast, spiraling galaxy or universe.

The following is a brief description of each of the Chakras. As previously stated, there are many excellent books that describe aspects of the Chakras in depth, so we don't feel the need to repeat that information.

1st – Root: Located at pelvic floor; Iridescent red
Front aspect: This is our basic, primal survival Chakra (tribal). It is instinctual and about our physical health and presence on the planet.
Back aspect: Holds keys to our unconscious beliefs about deserving physical life and well-being, regulates the physical system and flow of universal energy.

2nd – Sacral: Located just below the navel; Iridescent orange
Front aspect: The expression of feelings and creativeness with the world. Our connectivity to all others and our sexuality.
Back aspect: Supports the unconscious template of the front side. Supports us through changes and adaptations.

3rd – Solar plexus: Located at solar plexus; Iridescent yellow
Front aspect: The source of our self-esteem and self-power, our ability to succeed in the world. Our thoughts and mental structures.
Back aspect: Our mental templates of self and how the world works.

4th – Heart: Located at center of chest, near nipple line; Iridescent green
Front aspect: Love and ability to give and receive with others. Heart balances the lower and upper Chakras.
Back aspect: Connection to our heart's desire, unconscious belief about love and relationships with others and the Divine.

5th – Throat: Located at base of throat; Iridescent sky blue
Front aspect: Expression, communication, and creativity. Alignment of will and guidance from Spirit.
Back aspect: Access point for external spiritual guidance.

6th – Brow: Located at center of the forehead, just above the brow; Iridescent indigo
Front aspect: Seat of the mind, dreaming, intuition, and wisdom. Connection to higher levels of compassion and connection of all humanity.
Back aspect: Our potential and access to higher wisdom and vision.

7th – Crown: Located on top of the head; Iridescent violet
Front aspect: Seat of the spirit and truth. How we project our spiritual beliefs and programming. Connection to "knowing."
Back aspect: Opens us to the Divine, filtered by our belief systems.

8th – Gateway: Located several inches above the head; Iridescent silver.
Front aspect: Expression of your life purpose. Interacts with beings of different dimensions and planes of existence.
Back aspect: Expression of karmic and past choices influencing what you attract to your life. Work through past and future lives and visit parallel or concurrent realities.

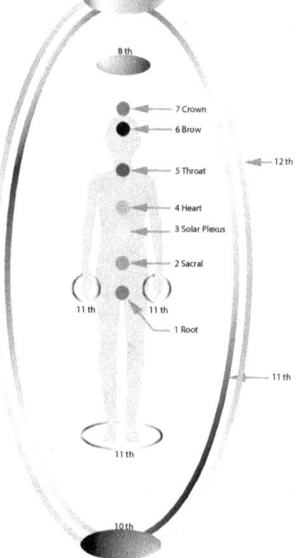

9th – Soul Star: Located 1–2 feet above the head; Iridescent copper
Front aspect: Projection of your soul's understanding of love. How you care for and connect with others.
Back aspect: Your soul's desires and beliefs about love and the world.

10th – Earth Star: Located several inches to a few feet into the earth below our feet; Iridescent earth tone.
Front aspect: Our interactions with the world and natural materials.
Back aspect: Aspects of the natural world you connect with. Ancestral lineages that you bring forward. DNA and epigenetic activations, both positive and negative.

The 11th and 12th Chakras are more encompassing and holistic in nature with the back and front aspects flowing together.

11th – Connective: Iridescent metallic blue. Dale associates this Chakra with the hands and feet as well as muscles and connective tissue. Our sense is that it is energetically intertwined with the fascial system. Fascia is electrically conductive and connected to every cell in our body. As such, it is part of the internet of the body.

12th – Golden Envelope: Iridescent gold. Connects all physical elements into the outer layers of the energetic shell that surrounds us.

The Human Energy Field (HEF)

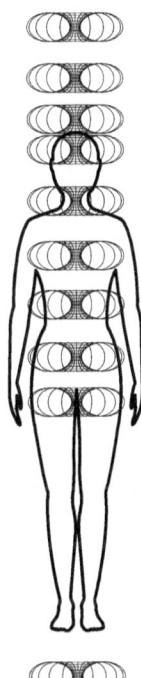

Our human energy field (HEF) is made of a series of torus-shaped fields that surround our entire physical body. Each field is associated with a Chakra. The figure on the left illustrates the first ten Chakras, each depicted as a spinning torus. Each torus creates a corresponding field surrounding the body. The fields are all axially centered along the central channel of the Hara. Each Chakra as we go up the numbers carries a higher frequency, which allows the field to extend further from the edge of the physical body. Some of these layers are composed of lines and grids (odd numbered fields: 1, 3, 5, 7, 9) and some are amorphous and more vapor-like (even numbered fields: 2, 4, 6, 8). The figure below, right, illustrates the toruses plus the 11th and 12th fields. A picture showing all twelve fields is too difficult to show as they all blend together.

The common 7 Chakra/Field model that most people use is workable, and our experience tells us it is pretty accurate, but it's only a partial picture. An inquisitive mind might start asking questions about the other Chakras. If there are more than seven Chakras, why would only some create fields? Our sense is that our HEF is actually more complex than the simple model would explain.

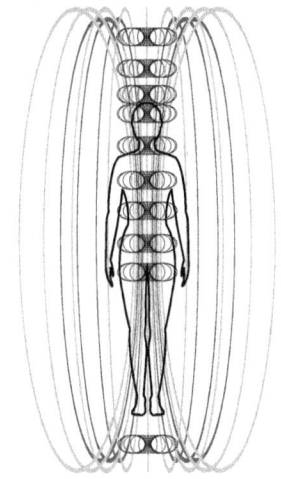

Our experience suggests that the 8th field is amorphous with a white or pearlescent glow. The 9th field is firmer, creating a shell-like structure. The 10th field is both amorphous and firm. As the

10th radiates up, it joins with the 9th creating an overlay that envelopes the body in an egg-shaped bubble. We find the 11th a bit more complex as it seems to create its own layer yet is interwoven as a web connecting everything in the fields. The 12th is again more firm creating a golden bubble as the edge of our field structure.

We don't think the field structure ends with the Chakra-related fields. Once we start looking at how we interact with the multidimensional universe, our soul, and group consciousness, things get more complicated. Our total energy body or Lightbody holds information and coding in additional fields and grids. In the next section, we will attempt to explain some of these additional fields or grids that are currently in our awareness.

Additional Components of the HEF

We preface this section with the disclaimer that we know our understanding is inherently incomplete and approximate. These additional components of the HEF operate multidimensionally and quantumly. Thus, most people, and certainly we, have a difficult time making sense of it.

The problem is our mental models of the world are built in the three dimensions of space (length, width, and depth) plus the fourth dimension of time. However, physics theories require additional dimensions for mathematical consistency in explaining our world. Various physics theories require either 10, 11, 26, or 33 dimensions for the math to work.

Our brains are not particularly good at conceptualizing things in 10 dimensions, and things really start falling apart as we attempt to visualize in 33 dimensions. Many times we have come up with models or explanations that we thought captured the ideas we were working with; however, when we run it by our guides for verification, we get an answer such as: "Well it is closer, but still not right," or more commonly: "You are trying to linearize the nonlinear—it is more complicated."

So we invite you to read what we have to offer as a glimpse into a multidimensional quantum world that is fascinating beyond our ability to comprehend. We sometimes get confused about whether something is a grid (more structured) or field (more amorphous), as some of these layers seem to be both or seem to shift between the two. In the end, however, perhaps it is not so important which one they are, as it is more important to acknowledge their existence. These additional components of the HEF, include:

- The Matrix
- The Incarnation Grid
- The Soul Field
- The Fascial Grid
- Other Organizing Fields and Grids
- The Primary Cell

The Matrix

When using the term "The Matrix," many are drawn to notions influenced by the 1999 science fiction movie of that title. However, the concepts of the Matrix presented by the movie have only partial relationships to what we view as reality.

In our thinking, the Matrix is a vast, fractal-like web structure that creates and organizes the universe or multiverse. What we think of as the "Grand Matrix" is the organizing consciousness of the Creator that pervades everything in all dimensions. We think of this matrix as carrying the instructions and organizing frequencies needed for every level of creation.

Within the Grand Matrix, there are many submatrices for each level of organization. The galaxy, the solar system, the planet, and each living creature have their own matrix, all of which interact with and are part of the Grand Matrix. The structure of our individual matrix contains the organizing principles, frequencies, and code to maintain our physical and energetic systems and guides us on our journey in this incarnation.

Our individual matrix is the underlying structure that holds the holographic projection of our Lightbody. When we work with the Lightbody, we are also working with the multidimensional interactions of the individual and the Grand Matrix.

The Incarnation Grid

We work with a grid or field we have labeled the Incarnation Grid. Our sense is that this layer contains organizing instructions and expressions that help us to maintain our earthly activities in alignment with the objectives and goals for this incarnation. Numerous clairvoyants and psychics have detailed accounts of a pre-birth planning process that we all participate in. We enter this incarnation with an agenda or outline of the people we will meet and the lessons we want to learn. It is not tightly scripted and leaves room for free will and experimentation. This outline for the incarnation is somehow energetically coded into this grid structure. We do not think of working in this layer of information as working in the Akashic Records, although there is possibly some overlap. At this point we have not been guided to use that terminology and have not specifically worked with the Akashic Records.

This grid communicates with our Core Essence, universal energy fields, and group consciousness to bring information and occurrences into our life that are in resonance with the grid's frequencies. Synchronistic meetings, sudden insights, and other supposedly "random" events can get organized through communication with this grid. Life events and thought expressions appear to create clutter or distortions in this grid structure. Sometimes completion of major goals or spiritual openings can create possibilities of new goals or realignment of the grid structure.

When we work with the Incarnation Grid structure, it is always with the help of our guides. The guides provide filters or cleaning hoops that we use to "comb" through the grid. Sometimes it feels as if it is just being cleaned up. Other times it feels that a new structure is being added. Greater clarity of this grid allows greater access for us to align with our life's purpose.

The Soul Field

Another field we have labeled and work with is the Soul Field. We have sensed that this field or grid is an organizing structure that mediates the interconnection of body and soul. Our sense is that there is a quantum-level communication connection to the High Heart. We use the term "High Heart" as an energetic structure in the physical region of the thymus, closely interwoven with the Heart Chakra and Soul Seat aspect of Hara. We work with this field in the same manner that we work with the Incarnation Grid. Using filters provided by the guides, we gently pull them through this field. Here, changes to the field are generally more subtle, but noticeable shifts in the field and connections can be perceived.

Within the Soul Field, we may unconsciously hold soul fragments of another person, or others may have left aspects of themselves with us. These fragments generally do not serve our highest good. So as the guide brings the filter in, we can invite all fragments we are holding to be released and returned to their sacred home. Additionally, we may have left aspects of ourselves elsewhere or have given them to another to hold. When the guides bring in the filters, we can invite all aspects of ourselves to return to us that are for our highest good.

Additional Fields and Grids

Most discussions of our HEF tend to focus on fields and grids that appear to be beyond the five senses, primarily because they are external to or outside the physical limits of our bodies. We also believe there are organizing energetic structures within the body. The generally accepted scientific theories place responsibility for operating the physical structure with our DNA. DNA holds the instruction set for making all the cellular and molecular components we need to maintain life. However, those theories omit the role of consciousness in the regulation of life.

Fascial Grid

One internal grid structure we work with is the Fascial Grid. Fascial tissue forms uninterrupted cellular sheets from head to toe. It weaves through and envelops every cell, organ, and body structure. The fascial tissue binds together structures, creates compartments to hold and transport fluids, and maintains our physical shape. It plays a role in almost every aspect of bodily function. Furthermore, fascial tissue is electrically conductive and may be the "internet" of the body.

We think that the true nature and importance of fascial tissue—and the Fascial Grid—is only now beginning to be understood by the scientific community. Recent years have provided a plethora of new discoveries related to fascial tissue.

We believe that the fascial system is an internal grid structure that is part of the electromagnetic HEF. Fascia may be the primary interface between the multidimensional aspects of consciousness and physical manifestation in this earthly plane. Our sense is that the Fascial Grid is communicating with the multidimensional HEF on a quantum level. There seems to be a strong quantum connection between the Fascial Grid and the Tan Tien aspect of the Hara.

Tim shares an account of one of his first experiences in sensing a distinct Fascial Grid.

> *This experience came shortly after my mother died while I was present in the room. My mother's Spirit/Soul had stayed around the room outside her body for a little over an hour after her breathing and heart had stopped. With a small ritual, she moved on, as most Souls do. It was after she left the room that my father asked me what I was sensing. So I walked over to my mother's body to sense and describe for him what I perceived.*
>
> *I sensed a distinct energetic field around the body that felt more physical than spiritual; it clearly was not the spiritual portion of her. I was curious, as I had never separated this field out from the rest of the HEF in an animated body. A sister that was present also confirmed this energetically.*
>
> *Then, a few hours after death, as family members were still in the room visiting, my sister noticed an energetic "pop." I checked, and the field had disappeared. Whatever was holding that field within the body had suddenly released.*

Other Organizing Grids or Fields

Our sense is there are many other fields or grids that comprise our energetic structure. As we evolve and ascend, we will probably gain greater awareness of the existence and importance of additional aspects of our energetic structure.

The Primary Cell

To best convey the idea, we draw on the concept of a Primary Cell from the works of Grant McFetridge and Cyndi Dale. The simple version of the concept is that at conception, our everyday sense of self is formed. All of that awareness is consolidated and encoded in the Primary Cell. Just after conception, the fertile egg that becomes us starts to divide. After the fourth cell division (16 cells), the Primary Cell forms. This cell stays somewhere in the body all our lives.

The Primary Cell resonates with the vibrations of the universal matrix to keep us in sync with our birth intentions. However, this cell would also obviously be encoded with the genetic makeup from our ancestors. Trauma in this life or our ancestors' lineage can cause epigenetic disruption to the cell. This trauma (past lives, ancestral, and present) disrupts the ability to fully resonate with our Divine plan. These disruptions create epigenetic shifts and can cloud the cell's communication ability and therefore our capacity to fully achieve our potential. Healing of the Primary Cell reactivates its ability to communicate and our ability to achieve our full potential.

When working with the Primary Cell, we find that it can be anywhere in the body, although it is often in the upper body near the heart. Prior to working with the Primary Cell, we take care to elevate our frequency and come from a grounded and loving presence. The process we have used involves holding our cupped hands above the heart area and inviting the Primary Cell to energetically come into our outstretched hands. Rarely is there any resistance from the client's Primary Cell. It usually jumps right into the palm of our hands, ready to accept the healing work. In the rare times it is reluctant, patience usually pays off as it comes to realize the safe, loving presence being offered.

We often will sense that the Primary Cell is obstructed by some sort of binding, trauma, or neglect. We have gotten images such as an old sea chest, wrapped in chains and barnacles. Or a cell wrapped in webbing. There are a variety of ways the cell presents, and occasionally, it is radiant. Usually, however, some level of cleaning and releasing is needed to support the Primary Cell to come into full radiance.

We ask that all binding and obstructions melt away. Once the cell becomes free and clear, we set the intention to gently move and activate the core DNA of the Primary Cell. Depending on the type of healing protocol being used, we fill it with light and let the specific intentions and frequencies of that protocol do the work. Our intentions are always for the client's highest good so that the Primary Cell is able to reach its full potential.

Chapter Five

Working with Personal Energetic Boundaries

Being aware of our own energy is of key importance to stay in a centered relationship with self and to be in a healthy relationship with others. The first step is self-awareness, as every reaction is about us and not about the other person. If you get bothered by another person, it is always an invitation to look within and explore what your energetic habits might be. When we can bring that awareness not only into the mind, but into the body and then the energy system, we can recognize more of our "wholeness." This heightened awareness allows us to release old energetic expressions and adopt new ones.

We each have an individuated energy field. This energy field protects us from the world and yet allows us to relate to the world and beyond (multidimensionally). As stated previously, we know that the energy field is an unseen aspect of who we are. This aspect regulates the inflow and outflow of energy that supplies the impetus to be fully manifest in physical form. We are energy, and we are physical bodies.

When you can notice how far extended or how close your energy field is in relation to your physical body, this supports a deeper understanding of how you interact with others and how you are feeling inside. Many times, you may pick up on another person's "stuff" if you are extended too far energetically. On the other hand, if you "run your field" too tightly or close to your body, you may tend to have less contact with the world around you.

Depending on their environment, sea anemones may become large when feeling safe, then when in danger or feeling threatened, they may "shrink" or pull in their body. It is instinctive for them. We, too, have instinctual and unconscious "motives" or awarenesses that regulate our energy system. We can support how we are in the world and what we choose to create by bringing our awareness to the conscious level of understanding.

Furthermore, our energy system can be regulated to support us more deeply. You can create less drama and trauma in your body and life as you bring your awareness to the conscious level. Your energy body can serve you just as your physical body can. Developing the skills to enhance and strengthen your energetic being can make life smoother and more joyful.

One of the tools we use in bringing awareness to assessing our own energy field is by placing a small hula hoop on the floor. Step into the hoop and consciously bring your field to the size of the hoop. Begin to notice what you are feeling. Some questions you can answer:

- When you stepped in, did you step to the front or the back of the circle? (Don't move, just notice.)
- Are you feeling safe in a circle this size?
- Is your energy filling the hoop in all directions? If not, where is it different?
- Are you comfortable in it? Is it familiar to you or foreign?
- What are the physical sensations you are having? Do you want to run away or sit down, or are you indifferent to it?

Stay in the hoop for 3–4 minutes. Write down what you noticed. Now try with a larger hoop and expand your field to the size of the larger hoop (you can also use a string for this exercise by making a circle with it). Revisit the questions above—what are you noticing? Stay in the circle for 3–4 minutes and write down all that you noticed. All of this information can support you in understanding how you are comfortable and what size energy field feels secure for you.

Awareness is key in learning how to regulate your own energy body.

We often continue explorations using the hoops. Experimenting with interactions between people using different size hoops or overlapping hoops can provide additional insights into how you manage your field.

As we work with an awareness of a more expanded energy system or HEF, including all the grids and fields and multidimensional aspects of ourselves, creating healthy energetic boundaries becomes even more important. As we work with raising our frequency, broadening our view of connecting at higher levels with our Core Essence, and transmuting trauma within the physical body, we tend to get triggered less and less by others "invading our space."

Chapter Six

Sacred Geometry and Color Elements

Sacred Geometry is an ancient concept that describes the unifying and organizing principles of geometric and mathematical expressions in our world. The energy of creation arranges and organizes itself in specific, repeating expressions. Consciousness or Divine principles create the underlying sacred geometric expressions of life. Each specific geometric expression has its vibrational resonance or frequency. The frequency of specific expressions can be used in the practice of healing arts. The frequencies of a geometric shape can aid in the shifting and moving of energy, helping accomplish the healing goal and bringing harmony and balance to the human energy system.

This section discusses some of the geometric expressions we use in our healing work. This book is not meant to be a treatise on sacred geometry. For more in-depth details, we suggest finding other sources.

Triads

The number three is associated with the trinity and completion. Three is often associated with wisdom and harmony. Biblically, and still in modern use, we often repeat phrases three times. We believe that there is power in the number three and find our work as a triad is much more powerful and fruitful than working in pairs or singularly.

Merkaba

The Merkaba is considered by many sources to be a Lightbody vehicle used to connect with and reach higher frequencies. It is also known to be multidimensional, allowing access to other planes of existence. It is

used as a tool by Archangel Metatron. A
Merkaba is based on a series of triangles.
Think of it as two entwined tetrahedrons,
one pointed up, the other down. Each tetra-
hedron is a pyramid with a triangular base.

We use the Merkaba in many ways. When
working with the earth and land, we visualize one or more large Merkaba bringing
in healing energy to shift local frequency.
We use the imagery in the body working with the Chakras and other
healing uses. We often visualize ourselves within a Merkaba while
meditating.

When we work together, we see ourselves as part of a bigger Merkaba.
Our triad becomes connecting lines, forming the base triangle and
connecting with Christ Consciousness to form the upper pyramid.
Our angelic guides connect to form the lower pyramid, completing
our Merkaba. The Merkaba is a powerful sacred geometric expression
that can be used in many ways.

Metatron's Cube

Metatron's cube is a sacred geometry symbol that has many meanings. The name is
somewhat misleading in that it is not really
a cube, per se, but a geometric pattern that
holds all underlying platonic solids. These
shapes combine to create all geometric
patterns of the universe.

The shape of Metatron's cube begins with
the geometry of the flower of life. To draw
the cube in 2D, take the inner 13 circles of
a flower of life pattern and connect the centers of all the circles with
straight lines. Those lines create the outline that we think of as the
symbol of Metatron's cube. In 3D, the cube becomes more complex
and contains within it all other platonic solid 3D shapes.

This symbol has long been a sacred symbol in Judaic and then
Christian artwork.

There are many interpretations of the symbology of this shape, which is said to embody the flow and balance of energy throughout the universe. It is used to represent the archangels, alchemy, magic, balance of masculine/feminine, and much more. We encourage the curious learners to explore the meanings and complexities of this sacred geometry by looking to other sources. There has been much written about this shape by authors more steeped in sacred geometry knowledge.

When we draw upon this symbol in our work, we visualize it as a 3D shape, usually spinning. We use the flower of life pattern as a protective shield, and we perceive the "cube" to be a tool wielded by Metatron to clear and heal our energetic systems. We specifically call upon Metatron to use this tool to repair and transmute flaws in our Hara. We visualize this spinning "cube" as a glowing and flashing geometric shape that slowly moves through our Hara, healing as it goes.

Labyrinth

Labyrinths come in many sizes and designs. Labyrinths have been found in numerous unrelated cultures dating to antiquity. The exact uses and spiritual meanings of the ancient examples are subject to much interpretation. Unlike a maze, the labyrinth has a single narrow path from opening to center, following a circuitous route to the middle. Many current uses of labyrinths are as an art form or an instrument for meditation and contemplation.

The energy concentration in a labyrinth depends very much on the intentionality of its design and construction, the frequency of use, and the mental state of the individual when walking it. Much like a church building resonates with the collective devotion of the faithful, a labyrinth holds the frequency of its walkers. We have found labyrinths to be useful tools to focus and quiet the mind in preparation for spiritual guidance. The slow, meditative walk to the center prepares oneself for an inner journey. Once in the center, we are prepared to open to guidance and communion with the spirit word.

Some of our best inspirations and information have come from sessions in a labyrinth. Franny built a labyrinth on her Colorado property. When creating any labyrinth, careful intentions in building, continued purity of thought, and sacred reverence creates an energetic form that allows that level of spiritual access.

Nautilus Spiral

We use the nautilus spiral as a tool to link human and Divine frequencies. The nautilus spiral represents a symbol of change and expansion. In nature, the nautilus keeps building new and larger chambers to encompass new stages of growth. So, too, does our human existence. We cycle back and forth, revisiting areas of difficulty in our lives. Each time, as we cycle into a new chamber or chapter, we can observe from a  different perspective and have an opportunity to learn. The growth spiral of the nautilus follows a logarithmic pattern similar to the golden ratio. We use the imagery of the nautilus to invite in the perfect Divine frequencies for our specific Lightbody and energy system.

Working with Color Frequencies

Color is vibration. In the color spectrum of the rainbow from red to violet, red vibrates at a more dense/lower frequency, whereas violet vibrates at a less dense/higher frequency, and the other colors range in between.

Each Chakra has a color associated with it which, in turn, holds that frequency. We can support our energy system by noticing which Chakra may be compromised and bring in that corresponding color frequency to strengthen a particular area.

In 2018, our guidance asked us to begin to work with a higher frequency of colors for the Chakras. As we listened, we began to experience the upgraded frequency of iridescence fusing with the Chakra colors. Red became iridescent red; orange, iridescent orange; and so on with all the colors. This shifted the frequency to allow for more expansiveness to the energy system.

One of the teaching tools is to experience and play with colors. Starting with your Root Chakra, bring red color into your hands and your whole being. Hold this color frequency for a minute or more, sensing and experiencing the color. Then, add iridescence and notice any changes. Try one by one with each of your Chakras with the appropriate color.

Rays or Ray of Light

"Ray of Light" is a title given to a specific or focused aspect of the consciousness of our Creator. The consciousness of the Creator pervades the entire universe. The various Rays of Light are different frequencies of the same one light: the energy of pure, Divine love that subtly guides and informs our reality.

In our usage, light is information. Each Ray is already part of our soul, waiting to emerge. The Rays are a form of teaching this information—they are a discipline or study of Divine light. Each Ray has an associated luminary or master. We can ask for the guidance of those masters and luminaries to assist in our work and our personal growth. One only needs to ask for their assistance, and they are ready and willing to help.

Crystal Grids

Crystal grids are an arrangement of crystal stones aligned in sacred geometric shapes or other alignments that serve to amplify the intentions for healing or manifestation. There are potentially an infinite number of possible grid arrangements. We do not consider ourselves the experts in this arena, as there are many other resources available to help deepen the knowledge for those interested. Our discussion here serves to describe how we have used crystal grids to support our work and in our client practices.

We seem drawn to the frequency of various stones and have plenty of rocks around the house. We find certain crystals or combinations of them to be beneficial for certain clients or situations. We rely on our guidance when deciding to include crystal grids in our workshops and retreats. Some workshops have included grids as part of the protocols, whereas other workshops have limited the use to experiential activities.

Often the crystal grids will be built with a center crystal and an array of supporting stones arranged in a pattern around the center. The center stone serves to both anchor and amplify the frequency of the intention. The surrounding crystals communicate with the center crystal and augment or amplify the center frequency. All crystals should be in alignment and supportive of the frequencies and intentionality of the work.

In previous workshops, we used crystal grids as an evening group experiential. This group activity allowed unstructured "play" time to allow participants to experiment and sense the energetic interactions with the crystals and grids. Through play, they were able to sense how the crystals shifted energy patterns in different arrangements. The groups were able to follow the wisdom of the stones in deciding arrangements. If attention is given to the crystals, they will show you how to arrange themselves.

Half of the workshop participants were participating via Zoom, and it was fascinating to watch how the groups of four, each in a different location, worked. They were able to make grids by "virtually" placing crystals in a grid. The grid held the energetic patterns every bit as well as the grids made by "in-person" participants.

Chapter Seven

Working With Spiritual Guides

Our experience of the natural world is similar to some of the ideas expressed in the theory of evolutionary cosmology. That school of thought believes that the entire universe is constantly in a state of evolution, rather than purely in mechanical motion dictated by the laws of physics, and that creative evolution co-exists within the laws of physics yet is guided by layers of consciousness.

Everything exists in nested morphic units, similar to a fractal. Whether it is particles, atoms, molecules, cells, tissues, organisms, societies, planets, solar systems, galaxies, or universes, at every level, things all exist as both a whole and a part of some larger structure or organization. Even respected physicists such as Rupert Sheldrake are finally starting to theorize that perhaps there is guiding intelligence at every level.

Our cosmology follows this train of thought. We believe that there are intelligent forces that guide all aspects of our creation. Those guiding forces, like all matter, are part of expanding hierarchies of organization, intelligence, and consciousness. All those levels of intelligence can be both the guide and the guided.

So, too, with us. As co-creators in our world, our spirits are quite powerful, yet we can access far more power if we tap into the vast array of guides at every level of creation. There are legions of angels, guides, and beings throughout the galaxy and universe. We are at once both a part of and the whole of this entire universe. Our evolution as humanity on this planet is deeply intertwined with the evolution of the entire universe. As such, much of the rest of the universe is rallying behind our growth and evolution. As we move forward, so does all of creation. For this reason, we have many helpers at all levels of the galaxy and beyond who are eager to aid if we would just ask.

The following section details some of the many guides that we are aware of who aid in this work. It cannot possibly be anywhere near complete as we are probably only aware of a small fraction of the many levels of guiding intelligences. As our awareness continues to expand, we keep getting pleasant surprises as more benevolent beings are revealed to us.

We want to add a note of caution here. There are many beings and forms of consciousness in the universe. We think of categorizing them in three different segments. Some are benevolent and eager to help humanity. Those in this group recognize the concept that we are all simultaneously separate yet a part of the whole. With that recognition, they know our advancement is also theirs, and they willingly support this common path forward.

Another segment is in a sense neutral, operating on their own agenda, unaware of our common oneness. Sometimes they are useful when our agendas agree. At other times they seem to be in our way, but they are just operating on an agenda that, at the moment, conflicts with our agendas. Perhaps one could think of them as competing for the same energetic resource, which they assume to be limited. One needs to be careful with this group as they could help today and hurt tomorrow.

The third segment (we think a small percent) are actively involved in working against humanity. This is as true in the human community as it is in other forms of consciousness. In the human world, we would not willingly share our credit cards with just anyone, only those we have determined will keep our best interests in mind. Much the same as working with humans, one needs to practice discernment when working with these beings.

We have found that the best way to practice discernment is to *only* work with those beings that you have discerned and/or identified are working for your highest good and that of all humanity. This is done by coming into one's heart space, being grounded into the Pure Timeless Earth, and connecting directly to Source. Then you ask that the information presented—or the beings that are bringing the information forward—is of the highest frequency of Divine light. Holding oneself in a high frequency state of being will support in getting an accurate answer.

We would like to make note here that *all* the benevolent beings that are helping with our work are of the Source/Creator. It is always our intent to bring forth the Creator's highest frequency of love— the Christ Consciousness light—in this and all dimensions.

Angelic Realms

This book is not meant to be a treatise on the many realms of angels. There are many other resources available to the inquiring reader that define the specific roles each of those groups of angels assume to aid as messengers of the Divine and helpers in this world. Similarly, there are many resources that give expanded details about any particular angelic entity. Note that we do not believe that angels have a gender. They may appear as male or female, and though we often use a gender-based pronoun, they are gender neutral.

We are only given a small glimpse of these guides and how they appear as they offer us assistance. They often show up how we want to see them or in a costume that makes us feel safe. It is our belief and experience that the angelic kingdom is at our service if we would only ask for help. All sincere and altruistic requests for help will be met with an instantaneous response. They seem quite happy to be of service and are honored that we ask for their help. They are bound by this request; however, they must operate within the limits of their rules of engagement and laws of the universe. Angelic and Etheric Beings are not limited by space or time and have the ability to be in multiple places or dimensions simultaneously. Additionally, they always respect the free will of humans to make good or questionable choices.

Specific Guides and Helpers

Christ Consciousness is the awareness of the presence of God/ Creator/Divine at the heart of everything in creation—every atom, being, plant, rock, animal, sun, moon, and all matter and consciousness. We hold to the value and heart-centered knowing that the Christ Consciousness is the purest presence of Divine love, gratitude, and compassion.

Janet Mentgen was the founder of Healing Touch and created a way to bring hands-on healing work to the earth in a more mainstream fashion. Her goal was to have healing hands in every home, school, and hospital. Her strong curricular program created the template of a 5-level foundational energy medicine program for the world. She passed away in 2005 and continues her work from the other side. Janet supports the Awakening Healing Axis collective by being a guiding light and teacher from the etheric realms.

Archangel Michael is mentioned in both Old and New Testament books as well as the Quran. He is portrayed as both healer and protector. He is often shown with a sword and in cobalt blue colors. We invoke his protection and oversight of our work. He frequently appears in his warrior form, standing guard in healing sessions or when dealing with difficult energies. His softer healing aspect is calming as he infuses that cobalt blue frequency through our nervous system. We see him as a constant companion in this work.

Archangel Metatron appears in Hebrew and Kabbalistic texts as one of the highest of the angels. He had a human incarnation as Enoch before ascending into an elevated status in the angelic kingdom. He is usually depicted with his sacred geometric form of the Metatron cube, which contains all the platonic solids, symbolizing the building blocks of life. He supports our work in a variety of ways, raising our frequency. We specifically call on him to support the transmuting and mainte-nance of our Hara.

Archangel Uriel is considered one of the major angels in religious texts. Uriel is the leader of the Seraphim and helps with healing resentments and forgiveness. Uriel shows in both gender forms and in red and golden colors. Uriel will step in when called and often appears waiting to be invited for those situations where that fre-quency can best transmute the stuck energies.

Archangel Raphael is known throughout most Abrahamic religions as the angel of healing. He is one of the archangels always invoked in this healing work. We see him associated with an iridescent emerald green color that can be used to open, transmute, and heal. We often invoke and incorporate the healing frequencies of Raphael's presence into the healing sequences.

Archangel Gabriel has a number of biblical appearances as the messenger of God and protector of truth and righteousness. We experience Gabriel as a strong protective force and a very soothing energy. Gabriel shows in both gender forms with an iridescent golden-yellow light that wraps us in warmth, love, and peace. Gabriel heals with a frequency of light, releasing, relaxing, and calming, and is also very useful in calming the nervous system and releasing traumas.

Archangel Raziel shows up in Hebrew texts as the keeper of the secrets and mystery. He is often depicted holding a sacred geometric form. We find him to be quite playful and joyful, bringing in an iridescent frequency of rainbow colors. He often operates as a cosmic level alchemist, transmuting any barriers in multiple dimensions. When we opened to his support, this work shifted into a higher frequency opening new doors. We often ask him to bring in the iridescent rainbow frequencies to clear and transmute.

Archangel Jophiel is considered the angel of beauty and wisdom. When working with us, she presents as an iridescent fuchsia frequency. She supports our work in holding a Divine remembering of the beauty and light that we each are directly from Source. Many times, she will appear with her fuchsia mist to surround and bring protection and stillness.

Archangel Zadkiel is considered the angel of mercy and leader of the dominions. He can be invoked as a healer for trauma and mental challenges. Zadkiel brings in the frequency of a deep, iridescent indigo blue. He serves with Michael as a leader in battle and captains the angelic Knights Paladin for protection and healing.

Knights Paladin is a powerful group of angels. They appear as male warrior knights. Some of us hear the sounds of their armor as they arrive. Usually 12 of them appear with Zadkiel when invoked, but at times there are more of them. They are a powerful protective force that can be called upon. They are also powerful healers able to transmute in multiple dimensions.

Magenta Warriors and Divine Dragon are a feminine counterpart to the Knights Paladin. They are powerful as a protective force and also marvelous healers. The leader appears often as a feminine warrior, commanding her band of iridescent magenta-colored warriors. They resonate with the frequencies of dragon energy and are amplified with the use of shungite crystals. We refer to the leader as the embodiment of the Divine Dragon energy.

Rahanni are a high frequency angelic and celestial group bringing in the iridescent pink frequency. They are a commanding presence when they arrive. They are great protectors as well as healers. When they are invoked, we often sense them come in suddenly as a powerful column of pink light. When protection is desired, they form a perimeter around the area needing protection. When invoked for healing and transmutation of energy, they are softer, yet power-fully transmute the energies and provide sustaining force to enable the healing to hold.

Ascended and Illuminated Masters support the work and the common ascension of humanity and the planet. The Ascended Masters are a collection of guides all having completed their incarnated work on the planet. They continue to learn and grow as they support us all in positions of the spiritual hierarchy. They all have specific areas of responsibility and work with certain frequencies. They will appear as needed and respond when invoked.

Another group that aids the work is referred to by us as the **Iridescent Masters**. This group of high frequency beings supports the iridescent frequencies and helps to maintain high frequency in our personal transformations and healing work.

Many Beings at All Scales help this work. From the atomic level to the galactic level, there are benevolent intelligences that are helping our common ascension. At the smallest scale we have been introduced to a group we affectionately label the **Comet Beings**. These beings zip around at the atomic and molecular level, look-ing like little comets. They seem to come and go as they traverse the multidimensional landscape of the micro-level world. They are willingly invoked to assist in transmuting energy throughout the physical body.

At the earth level, the cetaceans that roam the oceans are advanced intelligences that support the ascension of the planet and all her inhabitants. They can be invoked to participate in healing work and often transmute energy using sound vibration or toning.

The elemental kingdom of nature spirits is also a resource for healing. They can access many different healing frequencies. As in all things, discernment is especially important with this group as their trust in humans is not uniformly high. They have their own agenda and may not be in alignment with ours.

There are beings and intelligences available at the planetary and solar level that can be called upon when needed. These groups are especially useful when working with large scale energy disturbances related to space and time.

We have also been working with a group we term the **Star Beings**. They do not self-identify as originating in any particular star system. Their work has been related to bringing in a certain frequency of energy that we sense as a yellow-orange metallic color and high frequency. This frequency is particularly useful in working with the Lightbody and Matrix level healings.

There are many other galactic-level intelligences that come to our aid to create the highest frequencies sustainable in the healing work.

Guides and Crystals can work together to enhance the frequency. We have found a number of crystals to be useful for anchoring in and amplifying the frequencies of the guides. Shungite in particular seems to have opened a gateway into higher frequencies and associated helpers. Our sense is that shungite has been made popular in recent years as part of a grand guided plan to distribute it around the world, enabling a realignment of the planetary grid. The unique crystalline structure of shungite serves well to amplify the frequencies that are being brought in through this work.

When setting a crystal grid, we often start with shungite in the middle and then choose support crystals. Sometimes color is important in the supporting crystal; however, the basic defining quality is frequency. We have used a number of different supporting crystals. Black tourmaline is a favorite, along with quartz, varieties of amethyst, more shungite, and several others. The guides asked for several different stones such as anyolite, rhyolite, and dragon stone to support the "dragon" energy frequencies. The yellow amethyst (citrine) supports the "Star Being" frequency. Calcite has also been supportive for the higher frequencies and shifts in planetary alignment.

Chapter Eight

Role of the Heart in Healing

The heart is the doorway to the love we are all being asked to remember—to remember that we are the gateway to Divine remembering and connection with the Christ Consciousness. In all of our work, we focus on the power of the heart! The toroidal field that emanates from each person's heart expands and fortifies with greater force to strengthen us as humans living within a physical body.

The heart is the bridge between the physical and spiritual realms, inviting us to *be* the love of the Divine here in physical manifestation. It is through embracing the love of the Universe that we may be a clear vessel of light for ourselves, one another, and truly all of humanity.

All high frequency healing is done from a pure heart and Divine connection, allowing us to become conduits for love to flow through and with us as we work with the highest frequencies of guides and support.

The heart communicates to the brain and body through hormones. In 1983, the heart was reclassified as part of our hormonal system. One of the hormones, atrial peptide, helps to reduce the release of the stress hormone cortisol. As such, we have a chemical communication going on between heart and body all of the time. However, this is where things get really interesting. The heart is an electrical organ producing by far the largest amount of electrical energy in our bodies—40 to 60 times as much power as the second strongest organ, the brain. This heart energy permeates every single cell in our bodies. The signal is so strong that it creates an electromagnetic field (toroidal) that surrounds the body in 360 degrees and can actually be measured up to three to four feet outside the body.

When we increase coherence, stress levels go down, brain function improves, and we have the ability to feel positive emotions that regenerate us. This all leads to more awareness, intuitive discernment, and the ability to live a more heart-centered life.

Focusing the breath within the body, connecting to our heart, mind, Source above, and the heart of the earth allows us to be present and *be* that conduit for the Christ Consciousness. We strive to hold the template for each person and each participant of our workshops to fully remember that they are here to support themselves and the collective of humanity to bring about the great change we all have the power to contribute to.

Chapter Nine

The Making of a Workshop

These workshops and all previous and subsequent workshops follow a similar template. We believe it is important to ground our work in scientific principles and earthly knowledge, and to acknowledge the limits of this understanding. We then present our understanding, which usually goes well beyond the bounds of currently accepted scientific thinking. This is important as energetic work can only be partially explained by current scientific models, though it is also more than most people realize. Additionally, there are especially useful real-world analogs to energetic practices. Visualization is an important aspect of high frequency work, so it is important that we provide some platform of visualization to more gracefully allow the practitioner to make the leap into the multidimensional space of the high frequency work.

Workshop Preparations

Anyone who has put on a workshop knows that there is a lot of logistical work and planning that goes into creating a successful event. This work requires the same attention to detail that any workshop would require. In addition to the usual, we think it is important to take the time to energetically prepare on multiple levels prior to the workshop. We meet a few days prior to our workshops to make sure we have all the materials and presentations ready for the event. We also work to prepare the workshop space and the participants. Well in advance in the planning, we "visit" the retreat center grounds in our meditations and together during our phone conversations, preparing the land and working with the energies of the space to clear the area for our work. In the few days before the retreat, we again do guided work to open and clear the land. During our preparations, we have been visited by Native American guides that come to help us honor the land.

We also believe it is important to energetically connect and attune with each of the participants prior to the workshops. To aid this process, we ask each participant to send us a picture and write a page or so of background in response to some questions posed about the workshop. We take the time for our team to sit with each participant's paper and attune with them. In that process, we get insights into the needs of the various participants, noting that perhaps some subtle energetic shifts are needed. Most importantly, we are each more aware of what each person needs and how to be attentive to their energy and interactions during the workshop. We believe that the moment someone commits to a workshop, they energetically link up into the group and start preparing at a higher level of consciousness.

An excellent example was reported to Tim after a one-day workshop. A participant who had never met Tim said that shortly after she signed up, Tim began appearing to her in her dreams. Over several of her dreams, she was given all the information she would receive in the workshop, although she did not realize that was happening. The day of the workshop, she was in amazement as everything we taught was just as she recalled from her dreams. This level of connection and aware-ness may not be the norm, but we think that it is happening on a subtle level for everyone. We are always connected far beyond our normal level of thinking and understanding.

Labyrinth Ceremonies

We feel that it is important to start and end each workshop with a ceremonial ritual. The labyrinth seems the perfect vessel for that ritual. We always need to work with the local conditions and physical limitations of each labyrinth. Additionally, some places do not have a labyrinth. In those cases, we adapt the ceremony while retaining as much of the energetic characteristic as possible. Unique but similar ceremonies precede each workshop. The opening ritual has more than meets the eye and is designed to catapult the participants into the extradimensional space of the workshop.

As each participant steps into the labyrinth, they step onto the Merkaba symbol and repeat a phrase that opens an energetic door, shifting their energy system to be more receptive to the higher frequency teachings. Of course, each individual shifts in a way that mirrors their personal readiness and openness. Some who are fully ready are catapulted into extradimensional space; others shift more slightly. As they walk into the labyrinth, the group recites a mantra. Each workshop uses a mantra designed for the energies of that time. Many guides, representatives of the Native American elder's council, and elementals grace our presence and welcome us into the space.

We have a similar "bookend" ceremony to complete the workshop physically and energetically in the labyrinth. The closing ceremony is designed like the opening. Rather than opening to new concepts, the closing ceremony affirms and anchors the teaching. The participants all recite a mantra that is similar to the opening, although it is worded to be a fulfillment and embodiment of the ideas expressed. As they leave the labyrinth, they step on the Merkaba symbol and step out of the energetic envelope that held them for the duration of the workshop. The closing ceremonies are always filled with spiritual helpers, guides, and elementals honoring the light and awakening of all participants.

Sometimes participants are surprised to see how grateful and thankful the guides are. The guides are always eager to be of assistance, but seldom asked to serve in this manner.

Workshop Experientials

The following two exercises are included in the workshops to allow the participants to experience the power and frequency of forms that would otherwise be merely intellectual constructs. Most of us need to experientially sense something before we can understand it. We have found that this is especially true for energetic sensations that are beyond the normal five senses.

The Merkaba is a sacred geometry pattern, yet many people have no experience with this pattern. The torus is a common energetic phenomenon that is part of the human energy system, yet most are unaware of it. These exercises assist to make the patterns more tangible and to anchor an understanding of these energetic concepts.

Merkaba Exercises

As noted in the previous chapters, we consider the Merkaba to be an important sacred geometry element in this work. The Merkaba is much more than a geometric symbol—it is a powerful energetic gateway to accessing and using the higher frequencies available to us. Energy frequencies need to be experienced for us to remember and reproduce them. It is quite helpful to have an intellectual understanding, but it is only through the experiential that we gain the knowing that we seek.

The following describes the exercise we use to allow participants to begin to experience and integrate the power and energy of the Merkaba. Ideally this exercise is done in groups of seven. It can also be done in a group of four, although it is less effective. Facilitators not only direct the activity but involve themselves in creating the space, directing and amplifying the flows of energy for maximum benefit. The design of this activity allows everyone to experience the interior energy of the Merkaba as well as be part of creating the energy lines and flow of energy within the Merkaba.

Note: It is important to be aware that occasionally there are participants who find the energy too intense or have difficulty with balance while in the center. Using a chair in the center would be slightly safer; however, it puts the center person at a lower elevation than the rest of the group. We have had only a few such instances in multiple trials with this exercise. In one instance, a person with inner ear and balance issues could not tolerate the position in the center of the Merkaba and needed to stop. Another incident occurred where the person in the center dropped to the floor, unhurt, as they were caught by the group. In that particular case, it was actually healing. The energy was so intense that a non-beneficial energy that had been residing in them exited, causing them to momentarily lose balance.

The setup for this exercise is to create groups of seven. Ask one of the group volunteers to start in the middle position. The other six people arrange in a circle around them. The next step is to get every other person to hold hands together, creating sets of triangles. Getting people situated correctly for this part can be a little confusing. (See diagram on next page.) It works best if one person from each of the groups of three is then appointed as group captain to help direct the spin direction of the subgroup.

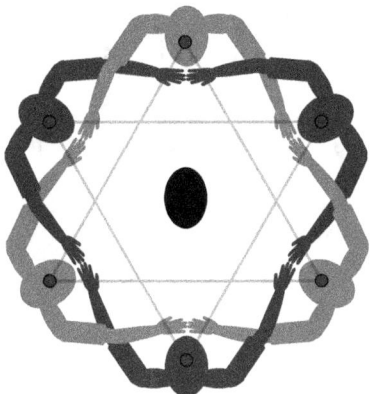

All of the spinning and energetic movement is created on the level of intentionality. The groups are not actually moving during the exercise. One triangle is asked to visualize connecting their triangle of energy with Christ Consciousness above. This creates an upward facing pyramid, which they will spin clockwise. The second triangle visualizes connecting below with the Divine Essence of Gaia. This creates the second downward facing pyramid, which they will spin counterclockwise (as viewed from above). Once everyone understands their role and energetic assignment, the group is directed to focus their attention on the creation of the Merkaba and spin in the appropriate direction.

This intentionality creates the energetic form of the spinning Merkaba with high frequency spiritual support. The person standing in the middle of the spinning Merkaba experiences the full energetic power of this dynamic sacred geometry. It is an excellent way to feel that frequency with the full body and get a glimpse into the power and potential. We use Christ Consciousness and the Divine Essence of Gaia as the two spiritual ends of the pyramids. Other guides or angels could be used as well. If the exercise is done as a group of four, then three spiritual helpers will be needed to complete the circle of six and create the Merkaba.

Allow the groups to experience the frequency and energy of the Merkaba spinning for 1–2 minutes. Then the group is directed to slow the spin and stop. Switch out the person in the middle. When the switch happens, be mindful of the group captain role, making sure each sub-group knows who the captain is. We find it best to switch direction of spin. The triad that was spinning clockwise shifts to counterclockwise and vice versa for the other triad. This gives everybody a chance to experience all roles and minimizes dizziness.

Repeat the Merkaba spinning experience for another 1–2 minutes. Continue the process until all seven participants have been in the middle position.

Follow up with sharing of the experience. Everyone will have a unique experience. It is fascinating to hear the different awareness of the energy and the range of experiences that are articulated. This experience creates a building block to energetically understand an element of the frequency shift process.

Torus Experience

We have used variations of our torus experiential as the last workshop exercise prior to completion. Having discussed the torus conceptually during the workshop, most participants have an intellectual idea of the torus as a fundamental shape of Chakras and energy bodies. As with most energetic concepts, true understanding is accomplished when we can grasp it both intellectually and feel it with our sensory facilities. This exercise creates a large energy torus with the group, which enables most participants to sense and understand the power and flow of energy within the torus.

Creation of the torus is quite simple. The group is divided in half. One half is directed to create a circle, holding hands together. This group will be spaced close to each other. The other group is directed to make a second ring, surrounding the first group. The second group spaces at arm's length apart. This arrangement now makes two concentric circles. Each group is then directed to create a flow of energy in their circle. The inner circle flows energy clockwise (as viewed from above), while the outer circle flows energy counterclockwise. This creates a large energy torus that is usually felt by even the least sensitive members of the group. The feeling is quite powerful.

The experience can be repeated by reversing the direction of flow and noting the difference. The inner and outer groups can also switch places and experience the torus from another perspective.

Chapter Ten

Basic High Frequency Shift

We always spend the first part of our gathering focusing on the High Frequency Shift of our energy system. This is an essential part of the work and a recommended daily practice. We believe it is one of the important keys to accessing the frequencies now available on our planet. These energy frequencies are new or have been hidden in recent historical times.

More energy frequencies are constantly being revealed as our human collective is quickly evolving and ascending. At first this may seem complicated as there are many steps to the process; however, with practice it becomes second nature and can be done quickly. When proficient, one can sequence through the steps in just a few moments. When we voice guide meditations for this practice, we typically take several minutes. It is good to periodically go slowly through it to fully sense and integrate the depth of energetic shifts at each step of the process. One may also realize that the more they practice, the deeper they go, and there are many subtle shifts in one's energy awareness. We sometimes feel nudged to slightly modify the order of steps in this sequence, so don't worry if you get them out of order a little bit.

- Invocation/Intention
- Protection
- Hara Attunement/Anchoring
- Vivaxis Transmuting/Healing
- Chakra Opening
- Hara Transmuting/Repair

- Core Essence Expansion
- Core Essence Elevation

Invocation/Intention

The first step is to invoke our spiritual guides. Include your personal guides as well as the angelic helpers. We invite in different spiritual helpers depending on the type of work we are doing. We almost always invoke archangels Michael, Gabriel, Raphael, Uriel, Metatron, and Raziel. In addition to these six, many others will be situationally called upon. It is also important to set the intentionality of the work you are doing, whether you are doing a healing session or just your daily energy hygiene.

The first level of intention we always set is that all will be to the highest good. This overarching intention is important, and it also inherently acknowledges that our conscious minds cannot begin to comprehend what that possibly means. Our limited understanding of "highest good" needs to be put aside to allow for the unfolding of a much grander plan. We may also have some secondary intentions— such as healing a physical or emotional challenge—that we can add.

Protection

The protection step focuses on creating sacred space within and around us for our work. The first step is to envision yourself connected to the Divine Source. How we do that can be very individual as we all have different notions of what Divine Source means. This needs to be your personal connection to "God," the universe, or some higher power. One simple way to visualize this is by having a power cord connecting us to the Divine. Just plug in that cord!

Once connected to Source, we visualize a coating of pure white light that flows over and surrounds us, covering us like paint. If working with a client, cover them with the same protective layers as well. Follow the white layer with a coating of iridescent rainbow colors. Cover that layer with a coating of gold glitter, sparkling all over you.

Next, we bring in an element of sacred geometry. Visualize yourself being surrounded by a protective bubble. The bubble has the geometry of the flower of life and shimmers with iridescent rainbow colors. We hold this protection in place as we work with the energy system of ourselves and our clients.

Hara Attunement

Attuning, anchoring, or setting the Hara activates that vertical line of energy that exists in the dimension of intentionality and focuses our connection to earth and purpose in life. We begin by putting our awareness at our Tan Tien in the lower abdomen. From the Tan Tien, visualize a line of energy connecting down to the very center of our planet. Imagine that you have your own personal, exceptionally large crystal in the core of the earth. Anchor the line of energy from the Tan Tien to your core crystal. Allow the frequency of Divine earth energy to flow up your connection, filling your Tan Tien.

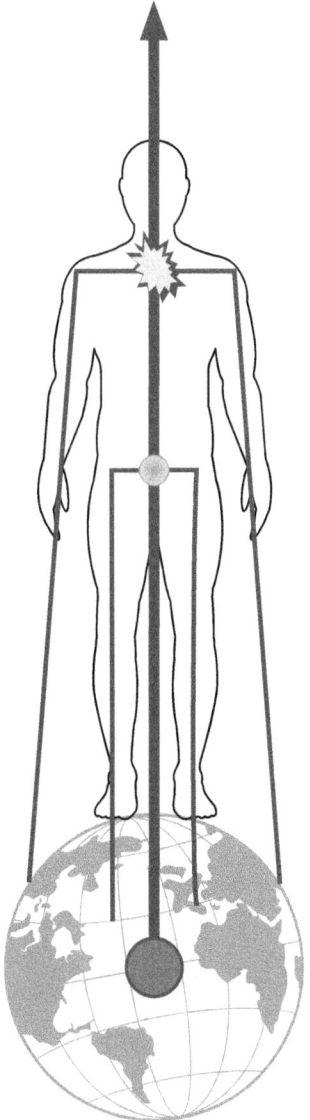

Next, bring your attention to the Soul Seat, located just above the heart. Draw that earth energy into the Soul Seat, then focus on a point above your head and allow the earth energy to flow straight up through the top of your head and connect to the Divine energy of the Universal Source.

Pause a moment to sense the connection to Divine energy both below and above. Visualize a column of light running vertically through you. Optionally, you may focus on expanding and strengthening the Hara connection. Expand by connecting the energy from the Tan Tien out to your hips, then down your legs, connecting deep into the earth. Sense your Hara column of light grow as wide as your hips. Next, focus on the Soul Seat, sending the Hara energy out to your shoulder joints and down your arms, connecting deep into earth. Pause to sense the feeling of a stronger, wider Hara, now connected by five lines to the core of the earth and the universe above.

Vivaxis Transmuting/Healing

Bring your attention to Vivaxis. Think of a hose-like connection from your left foot to a place in the earth somewhere near where you were born. Imagine a small sphere of light in the earth where it anchors. Sense the quality of that connection and the flow of energy. Ask your

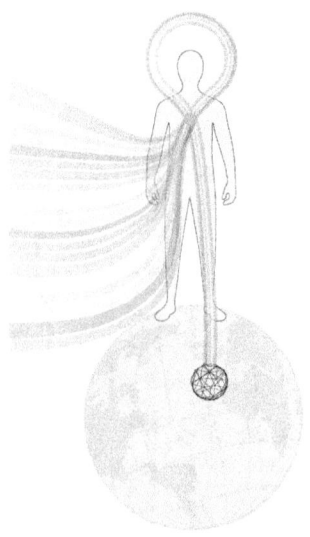

guides to transmute anything that distorts or blocks the flow of energy in your Vivaxis. Imagine it filled with swirling, iridescent colors of the rainbow or the colors that allow it to flow most freely. When that connection feels clear and flowing, visualize those colors flowing up your leg, dispersing into a vapor as they rise up your thigh.

Allow that flow of colors to swirl up across the left hip, through the torso on the front side, crossing the heart and up toward your right shoulder. The colors swirl around your head then down the back side, again crossing the heart and exiting through the entire right side of your body, connecting back to the earth.

This process may be slower the first few times you do it. With regular practice, you will find your Vivaxis is normally pretty clear, and it goes quickly.

Chakra Opening

The Chakra opening step focuses our attention on each of our Chakras sequentially. This focus opens and clears each Chakra, raising their frequencies as they open. We suggest using the iridescent form of the colors traditionally associated with each Chakra.

Starting at the Root Chakra, imagine a ball of iridescent red light flowing into the Chakra, spinning clockwise. Allow it to fill and energize the Chakra, spinning faster as it opens and clears. Allow yourself time to deeply sense the Chakra open, expand, and shift. Set the intention that it will stay spinning at that higher frequency.

Bring attention to the Sacral Chakra and visualize an iridescent orange ball of light filling the Chakra, flowing, and spinning clockwise. Allow the orange light to open, expand, and shift the Sacral Chakra. When it feels full, expanded, and rotating quickly, keep it spinning and bring your attention to the Solar Plexus Chakra.

See an iridescent yellow ball of light enveloping your Solar Plexus Chakra, flowing and spinning clockwise. Allow the yellow light to open, expand, and shift the Solar Plexus Chakra. When it feels full, expanded, and rotating quickly, keep it spinning and bring your attention to the Heart Chakra.

Imagine an iridescent green ball of light enveloping your Heart Chakra, flowing and spinning clockwise. Allow the green light to open, expand, and shift the Heart Chakra. When it feels full, expanded, and rotating quickly, keep it spinning and bring your attention to the Throat Chakra.

Visualize an iridescent sky-blue ball of light enveloping your Throat Chakra, flowing and spinning clockwise. Allow the blue light to open, expand, and shift the Throat Chakra. When it feels full, expanded, and rotating quickly, keep it spinning and bring your attention to the Brow Chakra.

See an iridescent indigo ball of light enveloping your Brow Chakra, flowing and spinning clockwise. Allow the indigo light to open, expand, and shift the Brow Chakra. When it feels full, expanded, and rotating quickly, keep it spinning and bring your attention to the Crown Chakra.

Imagine an iridescent violet ball of light enveloping your Crown Chakra, flowing and spinning clockwise. Allow the violet light to open, expand, and shift the Crown Chakra. When it feels full, expanded, and rotating quickly, keep it spinning and notice how all the Chakras are spinning and your energy frequency seems higher.

Hara Transmuting/Repair

We believe that Hara repair is best done by our angelic guides, and Metatron is our "go-to" guide for this work. Metatron uses the tool of his sacred geometric shape, Metatron's cube (previously described in Chapter 6), to recondition our Hara from the inside out. For this step, ask for Metatron's help. Ask that he transmute and repair your Hara to the best condition possible today.

As Metatron does the Hara work, you may experience different sensations as your energy shifts. Sometimes it seems that his cube stays in one place for a long time. This is usually in areas where the energy is not flowing well, and much repair work is needed. Envision Metatron placing his spinning cube into your Hara above the head. As the cube slowly descends your Hara, it spins clockwise. As the cube descends, you may sense that it moves faster or slower depending on the amount of repair work needed. It slowly works down the Hara column, out below the feet, and down to the core of the earth to the crystal where you anchor. Once there, it reverses direction, spinning counterclockwise as it rises through the Hara until it passes above your head.

The cube then reverses direction again and makes a second downward pass, slowly descending and spinning clockwise. The second pass is usually a little quicker as most of the work is done on the first pass. Occasionally a third pass will be needed.

After Metatron has completed the work, invite Archangel Raziel to fill your Hara with a tapestry of golden and iridescent rainbow light, infusing your Hara with the highest frequencies you can hold. Pause and sense your renewed and brilliant Hara.

Core Essence Expansion

The following description is a slower and deeper version of Core Essence expansion. We recommend that you periodically use this slow version as it allows for deeper clearing and heightened sensitivity to the amount of "stuff" we carry in our energy field. We do not need to carry that unnecessary baggage, and we can learn to travel lighter through our daily lives. In our recommended daily practice, you can move through the expansion in a few breaths.

Bring your hands over your heart space. Sense deep within your core being, connecting with your Core Essence. Imagine your Core Essence as a brilliant blue-white star deep in your body. Acknowledge that Divine spark that is your true self. As you focus on your Core Essence, visualize your star getting brighter and expanding into every cell of your physical body. Feel it light up your entire being.

Using your breath, as you exhale, continue to slowly expand your Core Essence beyond the boundary of your skin out into the first layer of your energetic body. Light up and clear your etheric body layer. As you inhale, imagine your Core Essence drawing back to a point of light deep within. On your next exhalation, slowly expand your Core Essence into the second layer, your emotional energetic body. Sense it light up and clear your emotional body. Let Core Essence dissolve all the emotional energy that you are holding in this body. Pause here for a breath or two, if needed, to fully clear this layer. Be aware of the calmness that comes.

Again, as you breathe in, imagine your Core Essence drawing back to a point of light deep within. Then exhale and slowly expand your Core Essence out into the third layer, your mental energetic body. Sense it light up and clear your mental body. Let Core Essence dissipate all the thought forms and mental energy that you are holding in this body. Pause here for a breath to fully clear this layer and sense the clarity of a revitalized mental body.

Breathe in again and draw Core Essence back to a point of light deep within you. Exhale and slowly expand your Core Essence out into the fourth layer, your astral energetic body. Sense it light up, clear, and vitalize your astral body. Pause here for a breath, if needed, to fully clear and sense this layer.

Breathing in, draw Core Essence back to a point of light. Exhale, slowly expanding Core Essence out into your fifth layer, the etheric template energetic body. This is the blueprint of your physical body. Let Core Essence light up and flow through all the lines and grids of this layer, clearing and vitalizing your etheric template. Pause here for a breath to sense the difference in this layer.

As you breathe in, draw Core Essence back to that point of light deep within. Exhale and slowly expand your Core Essence out into the sixth layer, your celestial energetic body. Sense how iridescent colors flood and expand your celestial body. Pause here for a breath to experience your brilliance.

Finally, as you breathe in one more time, Core Essence draws back to a point of light. Next, exhale slowly and expand your Core Essence out, fully expanding into your seventh layer, the ketheric energetic body. Core Essence lights up the golden bubble of energy that surrounds you. Feel your pure, full expansion and remember this feeling so you can come here often. Hold Core Essence in this expanded state.

Core Essence Elevation

Elevation of our Core Essence is a key part of accessing the higher frequencies now available. This description is for a slower version, which is essential at first and wise to use occasionally if you are able to put this in your practice. It has been our experience that once Core Essence is elevated, it is like unlocking access to the frequencies. Core Essence will tend to stay elevated if practiced regularly. If not tended to, it will drift back to our old normal.

Following expansion of Core Essence (previous exercise), bring your hands to your chest, holding them over heart space. Connect into that spark of Core Essence and visualize it moving to your hands. Slowly lift your hands with Core Essence up to the base of your throat, in front of your Throat Chakra. Let it stabilize at the throat and get used to that spot. As you hold your hands by your throat, create the image of a Merkaba in your mind's eye, about the size of your hands, in front of your throat. Invite Core Essence to come into the center of your Merkaba. Your Merkaba is the vehicle for elevating Core Essence.

In the palm of your hands is a beautiful Merkaba with your brilliant Core Essence in the middle. Slowly raise your hands up in front of your face until they are level with your Brow Chakra. Allow Core Essence to resonate with Brow Chakra. You may sense an activation and shift in your brow as an energetic rewiring takes place. New pathways form and energies rebalance to allow function of Core Essence at the brow. Just patiently hold the space until the process seems to stabilize.

Begin slowly raising your hands again, this time to the top middle of your head at your Crown Chakra. Allow Core Essence to settle in at the crown. You may again experience a sense of rewiring and adjustment as Core Essence adjusts to this new elevated location. Setting the intention that Core Essence stays above the crown, lower your hands to relax and allow your energy to come to a new equilibrium. Take notice of the elevated frequency and give your Core Essence permission to reside in this new home space.

High Frequency Shift: Client

Moving to the head of the treatment table (seated is easier), place both hands on the Crown Chakra. Focus on your own Core Essence, maintaining frequency as high as possible. Invite Metatron to come through you, spinning Metatron's cube and entering into the client's Crown Chakra, spinning clockwise. Ask Metatron to transmute and repair the Hara as much as possible at this moment.

Hold space and observe as Metatron slowly works the cube down the Hara, transmuting and clearing as he goes. Allow it to go slowly and let any flaws and irregularities be repaired as the cube moves down the body. You may feel the difference as it works through each Chakra and potentially any fractures within the Hara. Once it has gone all the way down to the feet, it will travel to the core of the earth, reverse spin, then slowly rise back up. Metatron may oscillate his cube up and down a few times to assure that the Hara is smooth and expanded.

Next, move along the client's body to near their Throat Chakra. Bringing your awareness to the client, visualize or sense where the client's Core Essence vibration rests. Most people have the Core Essence between heart and throat. If they have done this work before or have a strong spiritual practice, it may be higher. Gently invite the client's Core Essence to rise in frequency. Using your hands, encourage their Core Essence to move toward the Throat Chakra as the frequency shifts up. Partial movement is okay if it is slow to respond.

Holding your hands above the Throat Chakra, visualize lifting the Core Essence up a few inches. As it comes up, visualize a Merkaba forming above the throat, with Core Essence encapsulated in the Merkaba.

Slowly move your hands and the Merkaba up over the client's face until it rests above the Brow Chakra. Pause at that position to allow time for Core Essence to come to equilibrium at the brow. Many people sense a restructuring or rewiring that happens as the brow adapts to the higher frequency of Core Essence. When it has stabilized, again slowly move your hands to the top of the head above the Crown Chakra. Hold that position for a while to allow time for the crown to integrate and stabilize. You or the client may again sense rewiring or energetic shifts as Core Essence adapts to this new location. Set the intention that Core Essence can now reside above the crown at this higher frequency.

Chapter Eleven

Advanced High Frequency Shift

If you have read our previous work, pay extra attention to this chapter and the small but important changes to the Advanced High Frequency Shift (AHFS). As we acclimate our systems to increasing energy flows, the guides continue to make adjustments, allowing ever greater connections to high frequency energy. We consider all of these techniques to be a work in progress, making frequent tweaks and adjustments.

The AHFS is a higher frequency version of the Basic High Frequency Shift (BHFS) in the previous chapter. We think that it would be wise to practice and integrate the BHFS before attempting to work with the advanced version. We have been using that philosophy for participants, advocating use of the BHFS to acclimate the system before doing deeper work. Some can immediately dive deeper, but not everyone. In our workshops, we tend to add the upgrades step by step to entrain that upgraded energy into the participants' energy bodies.

Similarly, we recommend working with and experiencing the energy of each of the previous sections before upgrading to the AHFS. This is an essential part of the work and a recommended daily practice. We believe it is one of the important keys to accessing the highest frequencies now available on the planet. There are a lot of small steps to the process, and it may seem complicated at first. Listening to the guided versions of the AHFS on our website is a good way to get used to it without getting bogged down in remembering the steps. With practice, it becomes second nature and can be done quickly. When proficient, one can sequence through the steps in just a few moments.

When we voice-guide meditations, we typically take several minutes. When learning, going through it slowly allows one to fully experience and integrate the depth of energetic shifts at each step of the process. One may also realize that the more they practice, the deeper they go.

The biggest change we've made to the AHFS is our connection to the planet. Previously we used the concept of the "new earth" or transmuted earth to connect with. This allowed us to connect to the evolving or ascending version of our planet. There are many groups of people on the planet working on ascension. Most are doing good work, but in different ways and often with different messaging. When tuning in to this variety of work, it seemed like an orchestra out of tune. Not all are at the same frequency, so the "new earth" felt discordant.

We were guided to the concept of the "Pure Timeless Earth Template." This concept is the potential pure earth that resonates out of the pure Divine Matrix. Once we started connecting into the Pure Timeless Earth, the energies became purer and more elevated. We also found that some high frequency people who had difficulties connecting to the planet did better. These advanced souls could not connect into our distorted earth but could connect into the Pure Timeless Template of Earth. This has important implications when working with the flood of enlightened souls that are now incarnating. The Vivaxis connection is also shifted when the Pure Timeless Earth is substituted for the current earth connection.

Invocation/Intention

The first step is to invoke our spiritual guides. Include your personal guides as well as the angelic helpers. We invite in different spiritual helpers depending on the type of work we are doing. We almost always invoke archangels Michael, Gabriel, Raphael, Uriel, Metatron, and Raziel. In addition to these six, many others will be situationally called upon. We particularly also invite in the Christ Consciousness frequency/ energy for Divine support. It is also important to set the intentionality of the work you are doing, whether you are doing a healing session or just your daily energy hygiene.

The first level of intention we always set is that all will be to the highest good. This overarching intention is important, and it also inherently acknowledges that our conscious minds cannot begin to comprehend what that possibly means. Our limited understanding of "highest good" needs to be put aside to allow for the unfolding of a much grander plan. We may also have some secondary intentions for our session, such as healing emotional or physical pain.

Protection

The protection step focuses on creating sacred space within and around us for our work. The first step is to envision yourself connected to the Divine Source. How we do that can be very individual as we all have different notions of what Divine Source means. This needs to be your personal connection to "God," the universe, or some higher power. One simple way to visualize that is having a power cord connecting us to the Divine. Just plug in that cord!

Once connected to Source, we visualize a coating of pure white light that flows over and surrounds us, covering like paint. If working with a client, cover them with the same protective layers as well. Follow the white layer with a coating of iridescent rainbow colors. Cover that layer with a coating of gold glitter, sparkling all over you. We then bring in an element of sacred geometry. Visualize yourself being surrounded by a protective bubble. The bubble has the geometry of the flower of life and shimmers with iridescent rainbow colors. We hold this protection in place as we work with the energy system of ourselves and our clients.

Hara Attunement and Anchoring

Attuning, anchoring, or setting the Hara activates that vertical line of energy that exists in the dimension of intentionality and focuses our connection to earth and purpose in life. We begin by tuning into the zero point of the Pure Timeless Earth Template. We are connecting to the Divine template of a pure potential that may be in the emerging future. This version of the planet has the highest frequencies possible to align with our evolving human consciousness and our energetic ascension. It is also important that the core crystal we connect to within the earth is upgraded and polished, allowing the crystal to resonate with and hold the higher frequencies.

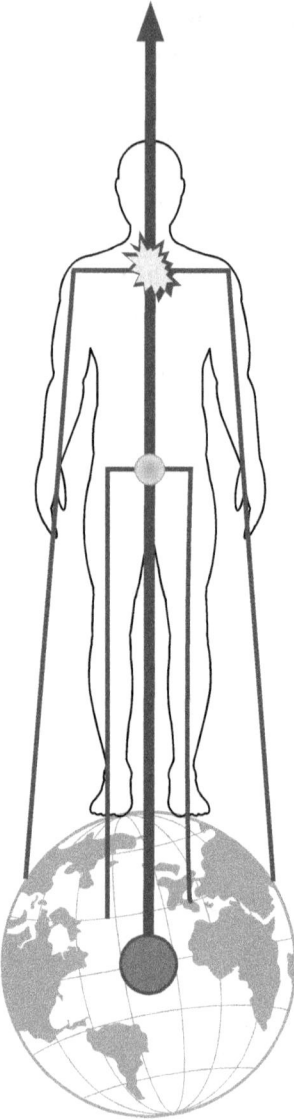

We begin by putting our awareness at our Tan Tien in the lower abdomen. From the Tan Tien, visualize a line of energy connecting down to the very center, zero point, of our planet. Anchor that line of energy from the Tan Tien to your upgraded core crystal. Consciously connect and merge your core crystal into the crystalline matrix of the Pure Timeless Earth. Visualize your core crystal aligning with the grid structure of this pure earth, becoming one with the earth. Allow the frequency of Divine earth energy to flow up your connection, filling your Tan Tien.

Bring your attention to the Soul Seat, located just above the heart, and draw that Pure Timeless Earth energy into the Soul Seat. Next, focus on a point above your head, allowing the Pure Timeless Earth energy to flow straight up through the top of your head and connect to the Divine energy of the Universal Source. Pause a moment to sense the connection to Divine energy below and above. Visualize a column of light running vertically through you.

Optionally, you may focus on expanding and strengthening the Hara connection. Expand by connecting the energy from the Tan Tien out to your hips, then down your legs, connecting deep into the earth. Sense your Hara column of light grow as wide as your hips. Next, focus on the Soul Seat, sending the Hara energy out to your shoulder joints and down your arms, connecting deep into the earth. Pause to sense the feeling of a stronger, wider Hara, now connected by five lines to the core of the earth and the universe above.

Vivaxis Transmuting/Healing

Bring your attention to Vivaxis. Think of a hose-like connection from your left foot off to a place in the earth somewhere near where you were born. Imagine a small sphere of light in the earth where it anchors. Connect the matrix of the sphere into the matrix of the Pure Timeless Earth. Sense the quality of that connection and the flow of energy. Ask your guides to transmute anything that distorts or blocks the flow of energy in your Vivaxis. Imagine it filled with swirling, iridescent colors of the rainbow or the colors that allow it to flow most freely. When that connection feels clear and flowing, visualize those colors flowing up your leg, dispersing into a vapor as they rise up your thigh.

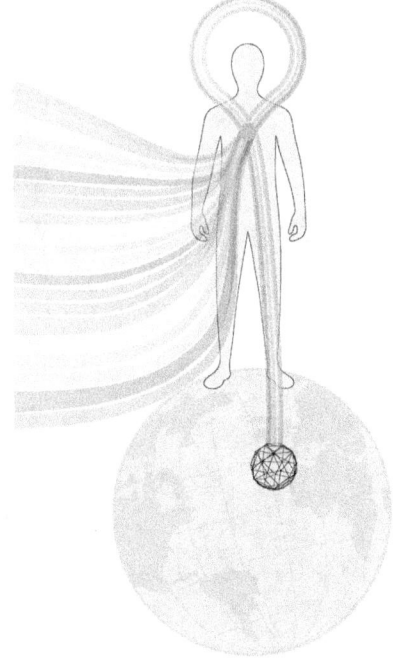

Allow that flow of colors to swirl up across the left hip, through the torso on the front side, crossing the heart and up toward your right shoulder. The colors swirl around your head then down the back side, again crossing the heart and exiting through the entire right side of your body, connecting back to the earth. This process may be slower the first few times you do it. With regular practice, you will find your Vivaxis is normally pretty clear, and it goes quickly.

When the energy flows more aligned, you may sense an

interaction between your Vivaxis and your 10th Chakra. The 10th Chakra contains information about your connection to the planet. As your Vivaxis expands with the gridlines and matrices of the Pure Timeless Earth allow a resonance with your 10th Chakra. Release anything in the 10th that does not serve your highest good.

Hara Transmuting/Repair

We believe that Hara repair is best done by our angelic guides, and Metatron is our "go-to" guide for this exercise. Metatron uses the tool of his sacred geometric shape, Metatron's cube (previously described in Chapter 6), to recondition our Hara from the inside out. For this step, ask for Metatron's help.

In this Advanced High Frequency Shift (AHFS), Metatron uses a

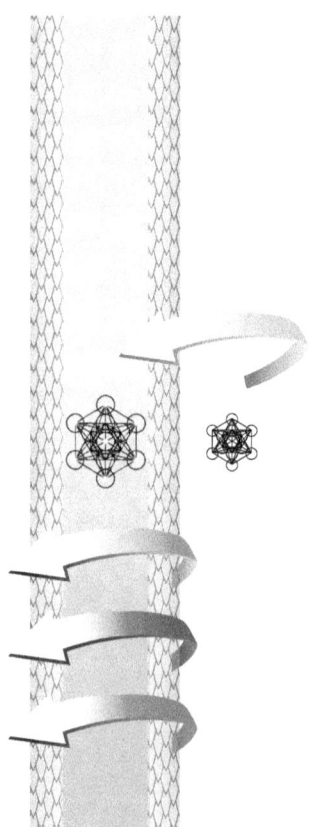

double cube. A larger version of the cube will descend through the inside of the Hara, rotating as it goes. A smaller version of the cube is connected to the larger cube. As the large cube rotates inside the Hara, the smaller cube rotates as it transverses the outer wall of the Hara. This combination of cubes repairs, renews, and transmutes the inner and outer wall of the Hara as well as all internal structures.

We ask that Metatron transmute and repair the Hara to the best condition possible today. As he does the Hara work, you may experience different sensations as your energy shifts. Sometimes it seems that his cubes stay in one place for a long time. This is usually in areas where the energy is not flowing well and much repair work is needed.

Envision Metatron inserting his spinning cubes into your Hara above the head, with the cubes spinning clockwise. As the cubes slowly descend, you may sense that they move faster or slower depending on the amount of repair work needed. The double cube slowly works down the Hara column, out below the feet, and down to the core of the earth to the crystal where you anchor. There it reverses direction, spinning counterclockwise and oscillating up the Hara until it passes above your head. The cubes then reverse direction again and make a second pass, slowly descending, spinning clockwise. The second pass is usually a little quicker as most of the work is done on the first pass. Occasionally, a third pass will be needed.

After Metatron has completed the work, invite Archangel Raziel to fill your Hara with a tapestry of golden and iridescent rainbow light, infusing your Hara with the highest frequencies you can hold.

Now that the inner work is complete with the Hara, the Magenta Warriors come in at the base of the Hara. Swirling clockwise with an iridescent magenta energy, they spiral up the outside walls of the Hara, polishing and cleaning. When they reach the top of the Hara, a Divine anointing oil flows down, coating the outer walls of the Hara, which creates protection and sealing of the outer structure.

Pause and sense your renewed and brilliant Hara.

Chakra Opening/Unification

Another up shift with the AHFS includes working with all 12 Chakras. The Chakra opening and unification step focuses our attention on each of our Chakras sequentially. This focus opens and clears the Chakra, raising its frequency as it opens. As the Chakra opens, it expands and flows into the Hara, unifying and blending colors into the structure of the Hara. We use the iridescent form of the colors traditionally associated with each Chakra.

Starting at the Root Chakra, imagine a ball of iridescent red light flowing into the Chakra, spinning clockwise. Allow it to fill and energize the Chakra, spinning faster as it opens and clears, fusing into the Hara structure. Allow time to deeply sense the Chakra open, expand, and unify as the vivid red becomes one with the Hara. Set the intention that it will stay spinning at that higher frequency, unified with the Hara.

Bring your attention to the Sacral Chakra as you visualize an iridescent orange ball of light filling the Chakra, flowing and spinning
clockwise. Allow the orange light to open, expand, and fuse the
sacral into the Hara. When the Sacral Chakra feels fully expanded
and unified, keep it spinning and bring your attention to the Solar
Plexus Chakra.

See an iridescent yellow ball of light enveloping your Solar Plexus
Chakra, flowing and spinning clockwise. Allow the yellow light to
open, expand, and fuse the solar plexus into the Hara. When the Solar
Plexus Chakra feels fully expanded and unified, keep it spinning and
bring your attention to the Heart Chakra.

Imagine an iridescent green ball of light enveloping your Heart
Chakra, flowing and spinning clockwise. Allow the green light to
open, expand, and fuse the Heart Chakra into the Hara. When the
Heart Chakra feels fully expanded and unified, keep it spinning and
bring your attention to your Throat Chakra.

Visualize an iridescent sky-blue ball of light enveloping your Throat
Chakra, flowing and spinning clockwise. Allow the blue light to open,
expand, and fuse the Throat Chakra into the Hara. When your Throat
Chakra feels fully expanded and unified, keep it spinning and bring
your attention to the Brow Chakra.

See an iridescent indigo ball of light enveloping your Brow Chakra,
flowing and spinning clockwise. Allow the indigo light to open,
expand, and fuse the Brow Chakra into the Hara. When the Brow
Chakra feels fully expanded and unified, keep it spinning and bring
your attention to the Crown Chakra.

Imagine an iridescent violet light enveloping your Crown Chakra,
flowing and spinning clockwise. Allow the violet light to open,
expand, and fuse the Crown Chakra into the Hara. When your
Crown Chakra feels fully expanded and unified, keep it spinning
and notice how all seven Chakras are spinning—with their brilliant iridescent colors flowing into the Hara—and your energy
frequency feels elevated.

Continue the Chakra opening process as you turn your attention to
unification with the 8th Chakra. Visualize iridescent silver light

flowing into your 8th Chakra a few inches above your head. Sense this Chakra open, expand, and fuse into the Hara. Keep your 8th Chakra spinning at a higher frequency.

Bring your attention to the 9th Chakra about 18 inches above your head as you visualize iridescent copper colors swirling into the Chakra. As it spins faster, it expands, opens, and unifies with the Hara, spreading the copper colors through the Hara.

Move your attention about 18 inches below your feet and imagine an iridescent earth-tone ball of energy flowing into the 10th Chakra, spinning clockwise. It expands, opens, and unifies with the Hara, spreading the iridescent earth tones through the Hara.

Shift your attention to the 11th Chakra as you visualize iridescent, metallic blue colors flowing into your hands, feet, and fascia. Feel the frequency of the 11th Chakra raising and fusing with the Hara.

Finally, bring your attention to the 12th Chakra as you visualize iridescent golden colors swirling into the outer edges of your energy body, activating and raising your frequency. Now, bring your attention to the unification of the energy of the Hara with all the Chakra colors and energies.

Core Essence & Hara Expansion

The following description is a slower and deeper version of Core Essence expansion. We recommend that you periodically use this slow version as it allows for deeper clearing and heightened sensitivity to the amount of "stuff" we carry in our energy field. We do not need to carry that unnecessary baggage, and we can learn to travel lighter through our daily lives. With repetition and practice, you can move through the expansion in a few breaths.

Bring your hands over your heart space. Sense deep within your core being, connecting with your Core Essence. Imagine your Core Essence as a brilliant blue-white star deep in your body. Acknowledge that Divine spark that is your true self. As you focus on your Core Essence, visualize your star getting brighter and expanding into every cell of your physical body. Feel it light up your entire being.

Using your breath, as you exhale, continue to slowly expand your Core Essence beyond the boundary of your skin, out into the first layer of your energetic body. Light up and clear your etheric body layer. Expand your Hara so it, too, fills the space of the etheric body.

As you inhale, imagine your Core Essence drawing back to a point of light deep within. On your next exhalation, slowly expand your Core Essence out into the second layer, your emotional energetic body. Sense it light up and clear your emotional body. Let Core Essence dissolve all the emotional energy that you are holding in this body. Pause here for a breath or two, if needed, to fully clear this layer. Be aware of the calmness that comes. Then expand your Hara so that it now extends out to the edge of your emotional body.

Again, as you breathe in, imagine your Core Essence drawing back to a point of light deep within. Exhale and slowly expand your Core Essence out into the third layer, your mental energetic body. Sense it light up and clear your mental body. Let Core Essence dissipate all the thought forms and mental energy that you are holding in this body. Pause here for a breath to fully clear this layer and sense the clarity of a revitalized mental body. Then expand your Hara so that it now extends out to the edge of the mental body.

Breathe in and draw Core Essence back to a point of light deep within. Exhale and slowly expand your Core Essence out into the fourth layer, your astral energetic body. Sense it light up, clear, and vitalize your astral body. Pause here for a breath, if needed, to fully clear and sense this layer. Then expand your Hara so that it extends out to the edge of your astral body.

Inhale and draw Core Essence back to a point of light. Then, exhale and slowly expand Core Essence out into your fifth layer, the etheric template energetic body. This is the blueprint of your physical body. Let Core Essence light up and flow through all the lines and grids of this layer, clearing and vitalizing your etheric template. Pause here for a breath to sense the difference in this layer. Next, expand your Hara so that it extends out to the edge of the etheric template layer.

Breathe in, drawing Core Essence back to that point of light deep within. Breathe out slowly, expanding your Core Essence out into the sixth layer, your celestial energetic body. Sense how iridescent colors flood and expand your celestial body. Pause here for a breath to experience your brilliance. Expand your Hara so that it fills to the edge of the celestial body.

Again, as you breathe in, Core Essence draws back to a point of light. Next, exhale slowly to expand your Core Essence out, fully extending into your seventh layer, the ketheric energetic body. Expand your Hara to the edge of the ketheric body.

Breathe in, drawing Core Essence back to a point of light. Exhaling slowly, expand your Core Essence into the field associated with the 8th Chakra. Now, expand your Hara to the 8th field.

Breathe in once more, and Core Essence draws back to a point of light. On your next exhalation, slowly expand your Core Essence out, filling the field of the 9th Chakra. Expand your Hara with Core Essence to the 9th field.

Breathe in, drawing Core Essence back to a point of light. As you exhale, slowly expand your Core Essence into the field associated with the 10th Chakra. Now expand your Hara to the 10th field.

Again, as you breathe in, Core Essence draws back to a point of light. Next, exhale slowly and expand your Core Essence out, filling the field of your 11th Chakra. Expand your Hara with Core Essence to the 11th and Fascial Grids.

Finally, breathe in and draw Core Essence back to a point of light. As you exhale, expand your Core Essence out, filling the outer layers of your energy body and 12th Chakra. Expand your Hara with Core Essence to the outer extent of your energy bubble.

Core Essence lights up the golden bubble of energy that surrounds you. Hara fills and expands into your entire energetic being. Feel your pure full expansion and remember this feeling so you can come here often. Hold Core Essence in this expanded state.

Bring Hara back to a size that feels comfortable to you. This may change over time, and it may be situational. Most people find that a Hara expansion of three to four feet feels right. If you are going out in public places, most people are better served by having a more compact energy body. Only if you have practiced good, clear boundaries should you have a large, expanded field in public places.

Core Essence Elevation

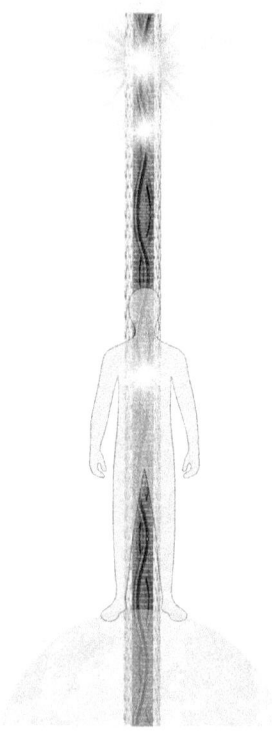

Elevation of our Core Essence is a key part of accessing the higher frequencies now available. This description is for a slower version, which is essential when first learning and wise to use occasionally if you are able to put this in practice. It has been our experience that once Core Essence is elevated, it is like unlocking access to the frequencies. Core Essence will tend to stay elevated if practiced regularly. If not lovingly cared for, it will drift back to our old lower frequency.

Following expansion of Core Essence, bring your hands to your chest, holding them over your heart space. Connect into that spark of Core Essence. Simultaneously connect into your Oversoul, which is resonating with the highest frequency of your soul in this plane. Visualize the connection between Core Essence and Oversoul. Let your Core Essence rise to the highest level it can reach.

Take notice of the elevated frequency and give your Core Essence permission to reside in this new home space.

Advanced High Frequency Shift: Client

The advanced version of HFS for the client is very close to the version described in the basic HFS section previously, with a few additions included. The first is to include clearing of the client's Vivaxis, which was not part of the earlier description.

When working with the client's Vivaxis, hold one hand on the bottom of their left foot and the other hand palm facing out below their foot. Focus on the sphere where the Vivaxis is connected to the earth. Ask the guides to help. Ask that the sphere connection be shifted to connect with the Pure Timeless Earth, which will give it a higher frequency connection. Visualize it connecting to the earth grids and crystal matrix of the planet.

Next, focus on the connection between the sphere and the left foot of the client. Work with the guides to clear any blockages or distortions. They may use any range of colors or elements to clear the flow. When good flow is established, check to see that it flows through the body optimally. Again, use the guides to assist as needed.

When flow feels strong, moving to the head of the treatment table (seated is easier), place both hands on the client's Crown Chakra. Focus on your own Core Essence, maintaining frequency as high as possible. Invite Metatron to come through you, spinning a double cube and entering into the client's Crown Chakra, spinning clockwise, descending down the Hara. Ask Metatron to transmute and repair the Hara as much as possible at this moment. You might sense that his cubes stay in one place for a long time. This is usually in areas where the energy is not flowing well and much repair work is needed.

The double cube slowly works down the Hara column, out below the feet, and down to the core of the earth to the crystal where the client anchors. There it reverses direction, spinning counterclockwise and oscillating up the Hara until it passes above their head. The cubes then reverse direction again and make a second pass, slowly descending, spinning clockwise. The second pass is usually a little quicker as most of the work is done on the first pass. Occasionally, a third pass will be needed.

After Metatron has completed the work, invite Archangel Raziel to fill the client's Hara with a tapestry of golden and iridescent rainbow light, infusing the Hara with the highest frequencies they can hold.

Now that the inner work is complete with the Hara, the Magenta Warriors come in at the base of the Hara. Swirling clockwise with an iridescent magenta energy, they spiral up the outside walls of the Hara, polishing and cleaning. When they reach the top of the Hara, a Divine anointing oil flows down, coating the outer walls of the Hara, which creates protection and sealing of the outer structure.

Next, move along the client's body to near their Throat Chakra. Bringing your awareness to the client, visualize or sense where the client's Core Essence vibration rests. Most people have the Core Essence between heart and throat. If they have done this work before or have a strong spiritual practice, it may be higher. Gently invite the client's Core Essence to rise in frequency. Using your hands, encourage their Core Essence to move toward the Throat Chakra as the frequency shifts up. Partial movement is okay if it is slow to respond.

Holding your hands above the Throat Chakra, visualize lifting the Core Essence up a few inches. As it comes up, visualize a Merkaba forming above the throat, with Core Essence encapsulated in the Merkaba.

Slowly move your hands and the Merkaba up over the client's face until it rests above the Brow Chakra. Pause at that position to allow time for Core Essence to come to equilibrium at the brow. Many people sense a restructuring or rewiring that happens as the brow adapts to the higher frequency of Core Essence. When it has stabilized, again slowly move your hands to the top of the head above the Crown Chakra. Hold that position for a while to allow time for the crown to integrate and stabilize. You or the client may again sense rewiring or energetic shifts as Core Essence adapts to this new location. Set the intention that Core Essence can now reside above the crown at this higher frequency.

Part 2

Spring 2022 Workshop

Ivoryton, CT

Clearing the Lens of Self-Understanding and
Self-Compassion to Facilitate Healthy
Relationships and Boundaries

Chapter Twelve

Creation of the Spring 2022 Workshop

We generally tell our guides not to feed us information for following retreats until we wrap up the retreat in front of us. We need to work in this linear world sometimes to keep ourselves organized. As soon as we wrapped up the fall 2021 retreat, we started the listening process to figure out what was coming next. Sometimes it all comes rushing in at once; sometimes it comes in dribbles. This time we also wanted to allow space for the expanded group of collaborators to have input.

We also wanted to change things up a little bit in terms of content. Our advanced workshops have been quite intense and targeted to people who practice healing work with clients. However, many attendees are equally interested in just the personal growth and healing aspect of the work. As such, we decided to shorten the spring workshop by one day and reduce the amount of table-based healing protocols. We thought this would appeal to a wider spectrum of participants.

Our initial thinking was that the focus would be on interpersonal communication, healthy interactions/relationships, boundaries, and how we hold ourselves energetically with those interactions. To answer the question: How can we create security as we navigate the energetics of personal boundaries and interactions? However, we also felt that self-love needed to be interwoven as it significantly influences all those concepts. Additionally, self-realization as a concept kept coming up, inviting us to consider how to keep expanding our potential as we shift our perceptions of reality. We also talked about the concepts of having filters of perception or mirrors of reality. As we considered all of this, images of stepping stones appeared. How could we create a path through these ideas accessible to both the beginner and advanced?

We worked as a larger team to focus these ideas and weave them into a coherent curriculum for the 20 hours of workshop time. The ideas of mirrors, filters of perception, and filters of self-love are woven throughout the program. We decided to include an exploration of the styles of connection, as our choices of expressing or receiving connection are influenced by the distortions in our self-love and the filters of our perception. We also wove together the concept of energetic security expressions with personal boundaries and energetic boundary interactions.

Ultimately, a mix of guided personal explorations, group interactions, and table-based healing protocols were crafted. This blend of activities allowed the participants to start down the stepping stone path toward understanding how their perceptions and energetic expressions filter and create their unique version of reality. With their new awareness and healing tools, they can take steps toward greater presence and realization of their sacred gifts.

Energetic Security Expressions

The energetic security expression work draws on multiple sources as well as our experiences. Barbara Brennan's work in this area talks about it as character structures, using Freudian labels that are not very attractive. We have also looked at John C. Pierrakos' work with Core Energetics. We found Steven Kessler's (author of *The 5 Personality Patterns: Your Guide to Understanding Yourself and Others and Developing Emotional Maturity*) work on the topic to be more affirming and supportive. His information simplifies things down to five basic character types, or personality patterns. We have shifted the terminology to better fit our understanding, energetic habits, and focus on the gifts of these expressions more than the defensive nature of the expression.

The basic idea is that as we are learning to survive in this world as children, we develop energetic expressions to deal with the parts of life that overwhelm us. Some expressions seem to work better than others, so we develop our favorite energetic responses to life situations. These expressions then become ingrained in our behavior. While the gift side of the expression may be very rewarding, the defensive side of the expression can become habitual and may be overused in situations that are not as threatening to our adult selves. We work with these expressions to deepen our understanding of self, allowing us to cherish the gifts of the expressions while reducing the unwanted side effects of the defensive aspects of the expressions.

Mirrors

The idea of seeing the outside world as merely a reflection of our inner state is based on the notion that how we perceive the world is heavily influenced by our beliefs and emotions. We incorporated some of the mirror concepts based on Gregg Braden's interpretation of the Seven Essene Mirrors. However, for simplicity, we only used five mirrors. The mirror concept suggests that our state of mind and spirit attracts situations and people into our life as mirrors so that we will improve ourselves. When we realize that the things in our life are happening because of how we feel inside, we realize that with some spiritual work, we can truly change our inner world and the world around us.

The idea behind the mirrors is basically the Golden Rule. The experiences life brings us teaches us to judge ourselves before judging others and unconditionally love others as we would want to be loved. We can take that one step further and express love to others as they would like to receive love, rather than as we like to receive love.

Journaling

We provided journals for each of the participants and encouraged them to journal throughout the workshop. We normally do this for our workshops; however, during this workshop, we allowed more time for journaling as the topics invoked deeper personal exploration and pondering. We recommend that you journal as you read this book. We suggest that you may also wish to journal or take notes as you read along, as we encourage you to undertake the same process of self-exploration. After each of the new sections or experiential exercises, take the time to make notes on your thoughts and reflections. This may allow you to dive deeper into your process of self-revelation.

Chapter Thirteen

Opening Invocation: April 2022

We began the workshop in ceremony, using the following invocation to set the frequency and intention for the following days. The ceremony included a ritual to join as a group and move into multidimensional awareness.

Clearing the Lens of Self-Understanding and Self-Compassion to Facilitate Healthy Relationships and Boundaries

I step into the template of the Pure Timeless Earth, fusing my awareness with the crystalline matrix of our planet.

I inhale deeply and draw its powerful energy into and through me, activating my entire being.

I honor the ancestors, elementals, and benevolent beings embodying and protecting this and all space. I am at ease in the security they offer.

I welcome shifts in my inner awareness as I remember my sacred self as pure love and invite that deep presence into my body.

I open my arms and embrace the Divine light of Source, letting it fill me and radiate from me.

I breathe in, opening and inviting new Divine frequencies of pure love to flood through me as I embody all aspects of my sacred self.

I release all limited ideas of self and reality. I open my heart and mind as an explorer, ready to journey into new perspectives of self and others.

I welcome the vision of understanding the mirrors of my existence.

I embrace new potential for awareness of personal boundaries and compassionate energetic interactions with others.

I surrender to serve the Divine plan, embracing the highest possible frequencies and dimensions flowing through me, allowing these frequencies to purify and amplify all aspects of my Being, accelerating self and planetary ascension.

My heart expands as I connect with the Divine masculine and feminine aspects of the Christ Consciousness and to my Oversoul as I awaken.

Workshop Experientials

The experiential portion of the workshop is where the amazing energy of high frequency does its work. Through these experiences, the participants have the opportunity to both give and receive the work. All of the following exercises are done as an energy healing trade. Participants pair up. One assumes the role of the practitioner while the other takes on the role of the client or recipient of the work. We refer to the person receiving as a client. When on the table receiving the work, powerful healing experiences can happen. Often, people have reported profound, life-changing shifts. The practitioner may also have profound experiences as a witness to the multidimensional healing energy flow. After the session is complete and time is taken for discussion and reflection, the participants reverse roles so that both have an opportunity to give and receive.

This exchange anchors in the frequencies and allows the participants to remember and reproduce the sessions after the workshop. Some participants have healing practices and will replicate the work with their clients, spreading the frequencies and healing. Others may be participating primarily for self-healing. Self-care versions of the experiences are provided for all participants, allowing them to continue their healing self-care at home.

Our intention is set for the recipient's highest good at this time in their life journey. This is guided work. We ask for the highest frequency level of guidance needed that will help the recipient today. These sequences have many steps, so it is best to have this printed material in front of you to help when first practicing until the practitioner can do it from memory.

Chapter Fourteen

Self-Love: Bringing Self-Acceptance Through All Levels of Your Being and the Mirror Image

Our Fall of 2021 workshop started with deep self-love work. This had such a profound impact on the participants that we felt it important to start with the self-love concept. The deeper we worked with self-love, the more clearly we realized that abundance or lack of self-love affects our entire worldview.

In the workshop, we began by weaving the concept of self-love with the concept of mirrors. We weave experiential exercises throughout this segment to slowly open the doors to deeper self-realization. Participants were encouraged to journal their thoughts and experiences throughout the workshop. We again encourage you to journal as you read along, too. We completed this first session with an experiential to explore personal sense of self and energetic boundaries. We continued to explore deeper into personal boundaries and mirrors as the workshop proceeded.

We began by exploring our sense of self using a handheld mirror. We suggested the mirror is a reflection of our self-intimacy ("into me I see"). We asked the participants to gaze into their mirror for at least a full minute, then journal what they saw, sensing and being present to what emotions they felt. We encourage you to put down the book at this time and do the same exercise.

We followed the mirror exercise with a description of the step down process of our incarnation. At our deepest levels of Core Essence, we are pure and vibrate with the frequencies of love. As our Core Essence lowers frequency to become Soul and ultimately our physical mani-festation, there is some distortion to the pure love. Further distortions get introduced as we navigate the world and create our belief system and worldview. That distortion affects our self-love and self-concept. The greater the distortion, the more challenging it is for us to express our love.

Ultimately, all expressions of our love get filtered through the lens of our self-love. If our lens is cloudy, less love is able to be expressed. A cloudy lens (low self-love) impacts all our relationships. It hinders beneficial thought expressions such as acceptance, compassion, and harmony. The cloudy lens feeds the low frequency thought expressions such as anger, pride, and fear. When we are low on self-love, we continually search for love outside ourselves. This perpetuates the illusion that we are separated from love. It hides the knowledge that we are, at our core, made of love; it is our true identity.

All this begs the question: "How do we clear and purify the lens of self-love?" If only we can clear the lens of distortion, we can align ourselves with the pure love that is our Core Essence.

We suggest that clearing the lens in personal transformation is usually a gradual process. A clear lens comes from embracing and accepting all aspects of ourselves with awareness and self-love. Clearing the lens means letting go of the false narrative that we believe about our lack of love. Lens clearing is not easy, as it requires acceptance and forgiveness of self. Many of us seem to be at war with ourselves, but we don't need to fight ourselves about the parts we don't like. A clear lens brings greater joy, love, and compassion for self.

To begin this process of self-acceptance, we asked the participants to slowly go through this set of statements as a mantra:

- I am my Core Essence, in oneness with Divinity.
- I am in alignment with my Oversoul, supporting me to be love.
- I allow my Soul to shine through me and guide me as love.
- I know that my earthly appearance is an aspect of love.
- I compassionately accept my human limitations, knowing I am love.
- I fill myself with grace to act in love.
- I lower my walls of protection to accept love.
- I am love, and I am being love.

We followed that with a guided meditation using the frequencies of gold to shift the more dense or lower frequency and entrain frequencies of love. Prior to the meditation, we gave the workshop participants an opportunity to sense and experience each of the gold love frequencies. The self-love meditation appears below. As you read this, allow yourself a minute or two after reading each paragraph to experience and sense the energetic frequencies.

Self-Love Spiral Infusion Meditation

Place your right hand along the right temporal lobe of your head. Place your left hand on your physical heart. Invite head and heart to connect, allowing heart to directly communicate with head, softening any mental resistance to deeply loving yourself.

Next, move both hands to be on or above your Heart Chakra. Visualize filling your Heart Chakra with rose-gold light… imagine white-gold light being added… and then pure gold—all frequencies of pure, Divine love. Allow those gold colors and pure love to blend in the heart, expanding the Heart Chakra and creating a golden bubble. You may see the sign of the trinity or perhaps even a Merkaba. Ask your heart to open to the frequency of pure love. Allow the heart to fill with this love, showering the earthly self with pure love. Sense this connection of self to Soul and Core Essence. Honor yourself as worthy of love, made of love, capable of fully loving and accepting love. Accept this gift of pure love from your soul, knowing that as your soul loves you deeply, you can love yourself. As your soul showers you with love, so do the souls of others around you. Allow your heart to be open to acceptance of the love from those other loving souls in your life.

Move your hands to your High Heart Chakra, bringing with your hands that bubble of pure, Divine trinity gold love. Allow the high heart to fill with this pure love. As your high heart fills, it connects into the seat of the soul. Let your heart and soul's desires be filled with this love energy. Feel your soul's connection to who you really are as a Divine spark.

Moving in a clockwise spiral, bring in the swirling bubble of pure trinity gold and your hands to your spleen. The spleen brings in life force energy (chi). Bring these pure love frequencies into your spleen. Ask your spleen to open to the life force frequency of pure love. Allow the spleen to shift, bringing in the life force frequencies that resonate with this love energy. Let your spleen fill the meridians and the physical form with pure gold frequencies. Let the spleen know that this higher form of life force is unlimited and abundant.

Continue the clockwise spiral rotation. Bring in the swirling, pure trinity gold and your hands to your Solar Plexus Chakra, the seat of ego and sense of self. Invite the solar plexus to open to this Divine frequency and flow of pure love. Let it dissolve away the old, limited sense of self. Let your real power and loving self shine through like a beacon of light. Honor your true self as a child of the Divine. Visualize that child held and lovingly caressed by a Divine form, loved beyond all measure. You are valued and treasured by the Divine.

Moving in a clockwise spiral, bring the swirling, pure trinity gold and your hands to your Throat Chakra. Invite your creative and communicative centers to open to that frequency of pure, Divine love. Allow your inner voice to proclaim the depth of your self-love. Let it give voice to your value, your ability to be love, and to love. Allow the throat to align with your soul and the Divine's will to express love in the world.

Continuing the clockwise spiral, bring the swirling bubble of pure trinity gold and your hands to your Sacral Chakra, the connection to all relationships. Invite the sacral to fill with this frequency of pure, Divine love. As your sacral fills, allow these love frequencies to flow out all the loving cords that connect you to other hearts in your circle of relationships. Fill those connections with pure, unconditional love. Let the gold frequency dissolve cords that do not serve your highest good, keeping only the loving, beneficial cords. Notice the love that returns along those connections. Expand your bubble of self-love, sending out love, noticing how the more self-love flows out, the greater the return flow of love back to you. Give gratitude for all the love you receive and deserve.

Moving in a clockwise spiral, bring the swirling bubble of pure trinity gold and your hands to your Brow Chakra, the seat of intuition and higher consciousness. Invite the brow to open to the frequency and flow of Divine love. Let that Divine love purify your higher thought processes and intuition. Bring your awareness to the connection with all of humanity. Feel your resonance with the collective love of the planet.

Continuing the clockwise spiral, bring the swirling bubble of pure trinity gold and your hands to your Root Chakra. Fuse the gold frequencies into the Root Chakra, allowing it to open and flow with the pure love energy. Invite your root to connect deeply into the earth, becoming aware of the security of the earth, sensing the soul's connection to the earth. Ask your soul to communicate its intention and strong purpose to be here and now on this planet.

Expanding the spiral, move the swirling bubble of pure trinity gold and your hands to your Crown Chakra, the connection to the Divine. Invite self-love to expand, feeling it resonate with the pure love of the Divine. Become aware of how the Divine responds and sends back more love than imaginable. Allow, accept, and become one with the love that flows from the Divine.

Let the swirling bubble of pure, Divine trinity gold love expand into all aspects of your field and self. Hold in your heart the profound connection to the Divine and the deep capacity for self-love you have experienced. Soak in the frequencies for a few minutes.

As a final step, coat yourself in white light. This protects and holds the energy, allowing time to integrate and assimilate the gifts of this session. When the energy feels integrated, become aware of your surroundings and imagine connecting deeply into the Pure Timeless Earth, feeling safe, secure, and grounded.

Next, we invite you to return to the handheld mirror. Gaze into it for at least a full minute, then journal about what you saw and sensed and what emotions you felt.

In the workshop, we then asked participants to join with a partner and spend two minutes just gazing at each other. This was followed by taking turns sharing positive descriptions of what they saw, sensed, or felt when gazing at their partner. They were also encouraged to share what they had journaled about themselves both before and after the self-love experiences. Again, we encourage you to put down this book and do the same exercise. If it's possible to include a partner, that would be a bonus!

Boundaries Experiential

This boundary exercise is intended to allow participants to become more aware of their own energy system while also providing an opportunity for them to become aware of and explore the energy system of another. The workshop included people with a variety of backgrounds and energy awareness, so we wanted to start with the basics. We gave participants a brief overview of the seven major Chakras and associated fields or aura. You have been given this information in previous chapters of this book. If you need to revisit them, we invite you to do so now.

The first level of exploration was with self. Participants were voice-guided through a sensory experience touring each of their Chakras and each of the layers of the field. They were invited to journal what they sensed. After a break, they worked in pairs and were guided through a sensory exercise where they took turns sensing each other's energy fields and sharing their experience with their partner. We encourage you to take a break and use your self-awareness to explore the current state of your Chakras and energy fields and journal if you wish. If you have a willing partner, you can do the described exercise with them.

Chapter Fifteen

Mirror Experientials

With the exception of the previous exercise, the mirror experientials are all described in the following section of this book to be more coherent. During our workshop, we introduced the mirrors sequentially over two days' time, allowing participants time for processing and some integration of the concepts before being exposed to the next mirror. Even though we think that it may have been a bit fast, we recognize that when in a workshop, the material needs to be covered in the allotted time.

As the team prepared for the workshop, we all listened to a meditation on each of the mirrors daily, one new mirror per week. That pace allowed for time to repeat the meditations and deepen our internal examination of the mirrors, providing more insight into how they are at work in our lives and perception of reality. We encourage the reader to come back to each of the mirror exercises after reading through them. Perhaps taking one mirror at a time and pondering it over a few days to a week for deeper understanding and integration.

Some of the mirror work was inspired by Gregg Braden's "The Seven Essene Mirrors" workshop. In our approach, we explore the use of mirrors in the self-love and energetic connections work we have previously created.

The First Mirror—Reflecting the Projection of Self

The first mirror was introduced with the following visualization, which was slowly recited for the participants.

Visualize holding both front and back aspects of your Root Chakra. Fuse the white-gold, rose-gold, and pure gold trinity into your Root Chakra, allowing it to open and flow with the pure self-love energy. Feel your Root Chakra connect to the earth. Feel the security of the earth, sense your soul's connection to the earth, and know it has your strong purpose to be here.

This first mirror is the mirror of the present moment. Today, be aware of what you see in others, which is really a reflection of what you are sending out. Notice what you see, such as joy, peace, anger, or fear. Experiment today with filling your root with love and security. Send out your confidence, security, and calmness. Notice what is reflected in this mirror.

The Second Mirror—The Reflection of What Should Be

This mirror exercise followed the break between sessions before immersing in the Divine Mind work.

Visualize holding both front and back aspects of your Sacral Chakra. Fuse the white-gold, rose-gold, and pure gold trinity into your Sacral Chakra, allowing it to open and flow with the pure self-love energy. Allow your sacral to fill with this frequency of pure, Divine love. As your sacral fills, allow the love to flow out all the loving cords that connect you to other hearts in your circle of relationships. Let the frequency dissolve all other cords, keeping only the loving, heart-connected cords. Give gratitude for all the love you receive and are worthy of back along these cords.

Notice any behavior in the people that surround you that causes frustration or triggers feelings of anger or bitterness, then ask yourself, "Are you showing me a reflection of self in the present moment?" If you can honestly say no, there is a good chance that it is showing you what you believe should be so and how others are not in alignment at that moment. Discernment is good; however, if we impose values on others and let that emotional charge energetically affect us, we will attract exactly what we dislike into our lives. Acknowledge we are responsible for ourselves, not all others.

The Third Mirror—The Reflection of our Hidden Gifts

The third mirror was introduced at the beginning of the evening session.

Visualize holding both front and back aspects of your Solar Plexus Chakra. Fuse the white-gold, rose-gold, and pure gold trinity into your Solar Plexus Chakra, the seat of ego and sense of self. Allow it to open and flow with the pure self-love energy, filling with this frequency of pure, Divine love. Let it dissolve away the old, limited sense of self. Let your real power and loving self shine through like a beacon of light.

The third mirror refers to that wonderful realization that happens when we see in others qualities of self that we have hidden away. We are energetically aligned and are drawn to them because we recognize ourselves in what they are projecting. It may be a part of self that lies dormant and unexpressed at the moment. Imagine a person that has that impact on you. See them clearly in your mind's eye. In the presence of this person, you may feel an attraction to something you can't quite define. When that happens, the mirror allows you to recognize those who have a particular "power" over you.

This mirror reflects something we have but have hidden, so we yearn to embody those gifts we see reflected. Ask yourself, "What have I hidden, abandoned, or had taken away from me that I can reclaim to be a full expression of self?" Ponder the answer to these questions. Bring yourself back into this moment and presence. Take a few minutes to journal about this mirror.

Think about this mirror the next time you have a deep attraction to someone that appears in your life. The answers may surprise you.

The Fourth Mirror—The Reflection of Compulsions

This fourth mirror experiential was provided at the beginning of the second full day, preceding the presentations on energetic expressions and styles of connection.

Visualize holding both front and back aspects of your Heart Chakra. Fuse the white-gold, rose-gold, and pure gold trinity into your Heart Chakra, allowing it to open and flow with the pure self-love energy.

Allow your heart to fill with this frequency of pure, Divine love, showering the earthly self and form with pure love. Sense this connection of self to Soul and Core Essence. Honor yourself as worthy of love, made of love, capable of fully loving and accepting love.

This fourth mirror has a different quality. It is asking us to observe ourselves, looking for our irrational, compulsive, dependent, or addictive behaviors. Through these feelings of compulsion, we slowly move away from the most important aspects of life, harming ourselves and those we love.

Is there unfinished business, something we miss deeply, or a life lesson we are avoiding? Some of these lessons could linger from previous lifetimes and lessons unlearned. Pause and reflect on this mirror of compulsions. What is being avoided or replaced as you engage in compulsive activities. As you feel into your body, sense, notice, and take notes. Journal about the experience of reflecting with this mirror.

The Fifth Mirror—The Reflection of the Divine Union

The fifth mirror was introduced at the beginning of the afternoon session before the group started working with trauma responses.

Visualize holding both front and back aspects of your Throat Chakra. Fuse the white-gold, rose-gold, and pure gold trinity into your Throat Chakra, allowing it to open and flow with the pure self-love energy. Allow your throat to fill with this frequency of pure, Divine love. Invite your creative and communicative centers to open to that frequency of pure, Divine love. Allow your inner voice to proclaim the depth of your self-love.

This mirror may stir us most deeply. The fifth mirror reflects our relationship with the Divine feminine and Divine masculine projected into our relationship with parents and authority figures in our lives. This mirror shows us unresolved perceptions of receiving love and support from our Divine and earthly caretakers. If we feel judged, unworthy, or inadequate it reflects our relationship with our Divine and earthly parents.

This fifth mirror allows us to recognize, discover, and acknowledge our beliefs and expectations, opening us to change what you believe. As you pause and reflect on this mirror, journal what you experience as sacred to you.

Chapter Sixteen

Divine Mind—
Love and Chakra Weaving

We created this experiential healing exercise to provide the participants with an opportunity to move more deeply into the frequencies of self-love, integrating mind and body. Prior to the healing trades, we gave participants additional information on the structure of the Chakras, including how we perceive the world through the front and back of the Chakras. We also showed them the concepts of the "zero point" of the Chakras. They were invited to tour and experience their Chakras and the zero point through a guided visualization.

The following script was used as a guided meditation for releasing and realigning the Chakras' back, front, and center points. We suggest you slowly read this and take time to ponder each part. Another possible way to experience this would be to record yourself voicing this as a guided meditation. Then play it back as you are in a more meditative state.

Divine Mind—Love and Chakra Weaving Experientials

In your mind's eye, state the following while continuing to observe the shifting of the energy as the releasing and restructuring occurs:

"I ask that any and all contracts, vows, agreements, pacts, arrangements, disruptions, unhealthy family lineages, and wounds that are not of my highest light at this 1st Chakra be forgiven and marked as complete, now and forever. Back, front, and center point." (Allow a little time for a pause as the energy shifts.)

"I ask that this Chakra come clean, clear, and current (pause as the energy shifts), and that it be brought fully into this timeline." (Pause as the energy shifts.)

"From the center point of pure potential, I invite my next expression of highest light to come into form." (Pause as the energy shifts.)

"I ask that a stabilization matrix be established at the back, front, and center point to best support me at this time, and that this Chakra come into cohesion with the rest of the energy system." (Allow a little time for a pause as the energy shifts before we move on to the 2nd Chakra.)

Once this is complete at the 1st Chakra, we move on to the 2nd, then we repeat the process and script at each Chakra (3rd, 4th, 5th, 6th, finishing with the 7th Chakra).

Divine Mind—Love and Chakra Weaving Healing Protocol

This exercise is done as an energy healing trade. Participants pair up. One assumes the role of the practitioner, the other the role of client or recipient of the work. After the session is complete and time is taken for discussion and reflection, the participants reverse roles so that both have an opportunity to give and receive.

The purpose of this technique is to:

- Activate the Golden Trinity and Divine Mind, integrating and permeating the purest form of Divine Love and Divine Mind, enabling the client to embody all aspects of their Divinity.

- Integrate the Pure Timeless Earth Template to charge and upgrade the Hara.

- Activate the back, front, and center point aspects of the Chakras for balance and integration.

- Fuse a strong sense of internal integrity, self-compassion, and personal strength for soul growth.

- Infuse the highest qualities of each of the 12 Rays of Light for soul evolution.

- Strengthen the connection of the whole energy system with the physical, emotional, and mental aspects of the person.

High Frequency Shift: Self

The first step of the session is Advanced High Frequency Shift (AHFS) for the practitioner. This is done while holding the feet of the client. The AHFS brings the practitioner to the optimum elevated frequency to be the conduit for the client. It also serves to entrain the client in that elevated frequency, beginning the process of healing.

High Frequency Shift: Client

The next step is to perform the client version of the AHFS, ensuring the client is also at an elevated frequency.

NOTE: The process for the High Frequency Shift for both the Self and the Client can be found in Chapter 11.

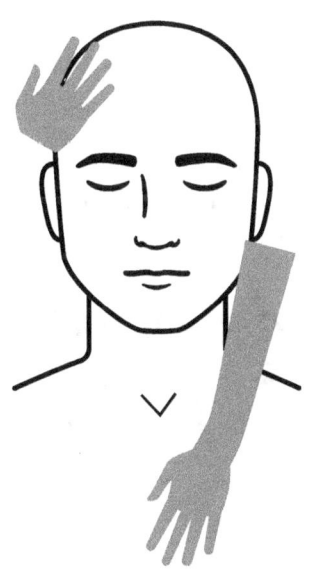

- The unique part of the protocol begins with the practitioner placing their left arm so that their hand is near the client's Heart Chakra and the client's head is resting on the inside of the practitioner's forearm. The hand is respectfully placed or held above the heart for female clients.

- The right hand cups the right side of the skull, with the thumb pointing toward Crown Chakra.

- The practitioner flows undulating energy between their hands.

- Invite the client to fully connect with their Soul, High Heart, and Heart Chakra, inviting pure, Divine Love, the Golden Trinity frequencies to flood into the client's Heart and High Heart Chakras.

- Next, invite Divine Mind to flood into the client's mind and brain.

- Hold these positions until you feel a full infusion of the frequencies of the Golden Trinity and Divine Mind. Allow the energies to integrate and permeate, activating the purest form of Divine Love and Divine Mind, enabling the client to embody all aspects of their Divinity.

Charging and Integrating the Earth Star/10th Chakra

Next, the practitioner moves to the foot of the table. Begin by visualizing the client's Hara. Visualize the Hara connecting into the pure essence of the earth at the zero point of the earth's core. Let the Hara connect into the matrix of the Pure Timeless Earth. Allow time to integrate with the pure earth core energy.

Through the client's Hara, visualize their earth crystal and Earth Star Chakra (10th) connected to the earth core. Allow the energy of the earth core to flow into the Earth Star, integrating and charging the Chakra. Allow time for the energy to fully charge and come to completion. When completely charged, visualize a sphere (ball of energy) six to eight inches in diameter generated at the Earth Star Chakra. The Earth Star Chakra is typically about 18 inches below the feet.

Asking the guides to assist, slowly allow the sphere of energy to move up the Hara to the Root Chakra. Hold at the root with the intention of allowing the energy ball of Earth Star to integrate with the Root Chakra, front, back and center. The integration charges, clears, and optimizes the root. Invite the client to embrace these words: **"I am woven into the fabric of the earth grids; I am safe and deserve a full and happy life."** Allow as much time as needed to fully integrate.

Activating the Chakras with Earth Star Energy

Continue the process with the assistance of guides by slowly moving the sphere up to the Sacral Chakra and repeating the charging and integration, front, back, and center. Invite the client to embrace these words: **"I accept all my feelings, and I stand in the power of creation and in communion with Source."** Allow as much time as needed to fully integrate.

Continue the process with the assistance of guides by slowly moving the sphere up to the Solar Plexus Chakra and repeating the charging and integration, front, back, and center. Invite the client to embrace these words: **"I fully accept myself, all my desires and experiences. I am a creator of healthy relationships as I live in harmony with all humankind."** Allow as much time as needed to fully integrate.

Continue the process with the assistance of guides by slowly moving the sphere up to the Heart Chakra and repeating the charging and integration, front, back, and center. Invite the client to embrace these words: **"I am fully supported and unconditionally loved by Source. I am Divine Love on the earth."** Allow as much time as needed to fully integrate.

Continue the process with the assistance of guides by slowly moving the sphere up to the Throat Chakra and repeating the charging and integration, front, back, and center. Invite the client to embrace these words: **"I trust the Divine guidance I receive and create the life I desire. I speak and embody Divine truth."** Allow as much time as needed to fully integrate.

Continue the process with the assistance of guides by slowly moving the sphere up to the Brow Chakra and repeating the charging and integration, front, back, and center. Invite the client to embrace these words: **"I attract and create my highest potential, fully connected to the pure earth."** Allow as much time as needed to fully integrate.

Continue the process with the assistance of guides by slowly moving the sphere up to the Crown Chakra and repeating the charging and integration, front, back, and center. Invite the client to embrace these words: **"I am the Divine spark of consciousness, fully integrated into my human form."** Allow as much time as needed to fully integrate.

Filling with the 12 Rays of Light

Move to the right side of the treatment table, place one hand on the client's High Heart Chakra, connecting deeply at their Heart and Soul level. The other hand is placed on the spleen, connecting into their life-force. Balancing Thymus, Heart, Spleen.

Invite in the 12 Rays of Light. Your intention is to support the qualities of each Ray to fill the Spleen, High Heart, and Heart, to support soul growth at the highest frequency of each Ray the client is ready to receive.

As a reminder, the colors of the Rays are listed on the following chart (sense the frequency of each Ray of Light imbued with pearlescence or iridescence):

1st Red	7th Violet
2nd Blue	8th Turquoise
3rd Yellow	9th Light Green-Blue
4th Green	10th Pearlescent
5th Orange	11th Peach
6th Indigo	12th Gold

Integration of the Entire Energy System

Standing along the right side of the table, set your intention to weave a lemniscate from the Earth Star to Soul Star, passing through the Heart Chakra to integrate, strengthen, and consolidate the entire energy system. (see figure below)

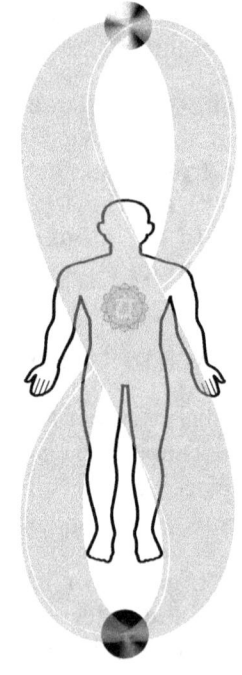

Anchoring Frequencies to Earth Plane

Move to the foot of the table. Holding the palms of your hands on the soles of the feet, visualize a plasma with rich, iridescent neon orange energy pouring from the palms of your hands. Allow it to flow into every cell of the body—the bones, fascia, muscles, organs, and template of the body as well as all the fields.

Next, allow the energy of the iridescent neon orange to come up from the earth through the Vivaxis to facilitate additional grounding and support these frequencies. This will support grounding and anchoring all the shifts to support the physical form.

Completion

As a final step, the practitioner visualizes streamers of gossamer threads woven and infused with iridescent diamonds, swirling around and creating a three-inch-thick cocoon of energy around the client. This protects and holds the energy, allowing time to integrate and assimilate the gifts of the session.

Chapter Seventeen

Energetic Expressions

This section provides information about how we view and experience reality and introduces the concepts of energetic security expressions. We were inspired by the work of authors Barbara Ann Brennan (*Light Emerging*), John C. Pierrakos M.D. (*Core Energetics*), and Steven Kessler (*The 5 Personality Patterns*) on this topic and built on it to align with the high frequency work AHA does. For a much deeper study of the safety patterns, we would recommend reading Steven Kessler's book. The personality patterns and personality types discussed by previous authors seem more rigid and physical. We adapted the work to focus on the more fluidic behavior of energetic expression and connections.

It is important to begin with the understanding that reality is not real. That statement may seem to turn the world upside down. The truth is that everybody lives in their own reality. We have varying degrees of overlap or shared versions of reality. Therefore, it is puzzling as we notice that some people have such different views of the world. We all have a hard time understanding others when there is little overlap or shared reality. Groups and cultures strive to reinforce the overlapping elements of reality for greater social cohesion. All our experiences, thoughts, and actions in the world are filtered in one way or another through our perceptions of reality.

Energetic Security Expressions, Filters, and Mirror Reflections

The diagram below is a flow chart, but you can start anywhere as it loops continuously. If we begin with the energetic security expression, our preferred expression (or filters) affects what we decide is important and where we put our focus. There is far too much information in the world to take it all in, so to avoid overload, we limit our information intake to where we place our focus. As a result, we perceive the world around us with that limited or filtered intake of information.

How we recognize the world is very much constrained or distorted by this limitation. How we now recognize the world defines our experience, which we identify as reality. Two people can partake in the exact same physical act yet experience it completely differently. Our perceived reality then allows us to create assumptions about how we think the world works. Our assumptions then shape our need to feel secure. We adjust our energetic security expressions so that we feel secure in the reality that we have created.

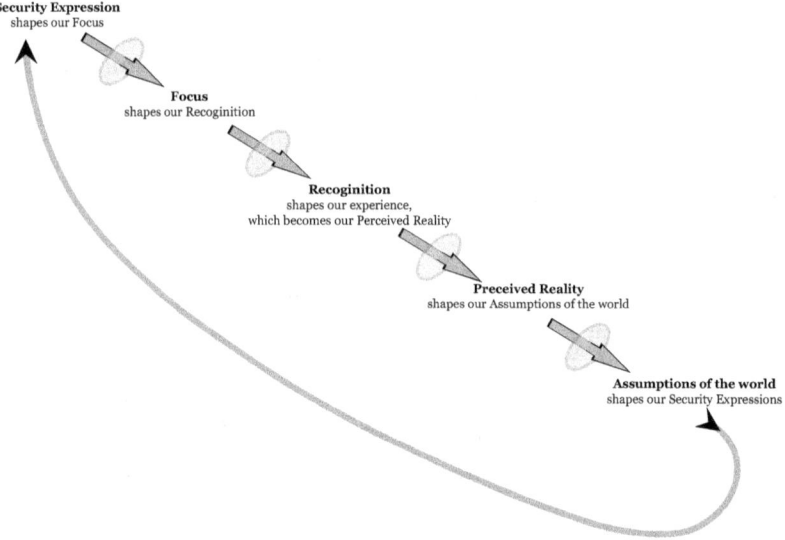

Security Expression
shapes our Focus

Focus
shapes our Recoginition

Recoginition
shapes our experience,
which becomes our Perceived Reality

Preceived Reality
shapes our Assumptions of the world

Assumptions of the world
shapes our Security Expressions

This constant loop shifts our reality throughout our lives as our filters get cleared or more distorted. Those with the clearest filters have a reality that is closer to real.

Energetic Security Expressions

We all have energetic security expressions that help us cope with the world and those around us. We each utilize some of each expression, but with preferences to certain expressions that we believe serve us best or once served us well. These expressions and preferences began developing early in our life based on our personality and the environment. Our belief systems and learned behaviors, as well as what we viewed as positive or negative, influenced these expressions and continues to do so.

Security expressions are all part of essential strategies for us to navigate the unpredictable world around us. The security expressions primarily come into play when we are in distress or feeling overwhelmed. The security expressions are more fluid than personality types, and we all utilize some aspects of each expression. The key to understanding the expressions is to become aware of how we respond to stressful and overwhelming situations. Each of the expressions has many gifts, so it is also important to consider the gifts of each expression and focus on how those gifts can enrich our lives.

We can consider these expressions to be part of the soul's work. It is something we do, not something we are. Like all behaviors, they can be modified. Thinking of it as our soul's work helps to stop blaming self and others. It isn't something our parents or some others "did to us." It is all part of our soul's plan to learn lessons and can span many lives. It is important to take ownership of the plan, as it shifts us out of the victim perspective and enables us to accept our situation and move forward more productively. Although it is sometimes hard to fathom why we are in a given situation, a soul gains empathy for others by experiencing the depth of unfortunate situations.

Childhood circumstances and relationships along with our soul's plan set up early energetic expressions, which can become a habit that might seem to lock us into a way of being. These energetic expressions affect our beliefs and ideas of how we think and feel. They affect how we experience our energetic and physical bodies and may even influence the development of our physical structure.

We believe that learning about security expressions can be an invitation to examine our self-images and belief system. This examination can lead to recognizing where our images and beliefs have been distorted in the past. Sometimes that distortion is merely the product of a very immature and incomplete worldview that a young child would hold. If we do the inner work of exploring and recognizing the expression, we have the opportunity to clear those old disruptions or trauma. That clearing paves the way to recognize and resonate with the gifts of our expressions. As we grow and our worldview shifts, our predominant expressions may soften, and it may be harder to identify with certain expressions. Alternatively, some may experience a deepening of the expressions if life circumstances amplify the beliefs and there is little inner growth work. We believe that no matter where you land on that spectrum, it is never too late to start the exploration.

We may find that particular people or relationships provide triggers for expressions that are the most challenging. In fact, stressful situations with those closest to us can often be the most challenging. It seems paradoxical that those who we hold most dearly can also present our biggest challenges. Of course, sometimes the trigger can also be with people who are strangers and may perhaps be more of a threat to our security.

Ultimately, the goal is to bring balance with all the energetic expressions and be able to enjoy the gifts and strengths of each expression while minimizing their unfavorable reactive aspects.

Energetic Security Expressions as a Mirror

Our energetic security expressions are both a filter and a mirror. As a filter, they limit the ability to express our true essence. Our Core Essence is the essence and vibration of love. This expression of love is filtered through the distortions of our security expressions. Our outward expression of love in the world is diminished by the expressions that are built upon false beliefs and limited thinking. Our goal should be to clear these filters to allow our true nature of love to shine through.

We can think of the security expression as a mirror reflection. The security expression causes us to see the world through the lens of that expression. If we make that expression a mirror reflection, we can begin to realize that what we see in others is actually the reflection of ourselves. We are constantly projecting our reality onto others, so what we see in them is really ourselves. This is difficult to do on a continual basis and is not 100 percent accurate. All people in the world are not acting for our sole benefit, so we need to use discernment when evaluating mirror projections. We can start by observing ourselves more than others. It is not the situation we have to observe, it is our reaction to the situation. How we react in any situation is based on our beliefs, filters, expressions, and history.

As we self-observe through the mirror of others, it is imperative that we be compassionate with ourselves. It is important to reinforce our self-love and unconditionally embrace and accept ourselves as we do this observation to avoid spiraling into self-depreciation and loathing. At first it can be a little shocking to realize that what we often dislike or are most irritated about in others is actually a form of reflection of self. Rather than jumping to defining ourselves by what we see, we can pause and ask ourselves some questions, such as:

- Is what I am observing something that I am currently expressing?

- Is what I am observing something that I may be judging?

- Is what I am observing something that I lost?

- Is what I am observing something that I am missing from my experience?

- What inner healing expression that is illuminating in me am I being invited to see?

- Is this being presented so that I can understand my own particular expression?

If we can observe from a place of deep presence, we can see in others and ourselves what we have never imagined. We will see the reflection of their Core Essence, reminding and reflecting who we truly are!

Skills to Support All Expression Types

The following skills are useful to support each of us as we learn to understand and work with our unique mix of security expressions. We gave participants time to practice and become aware of how these skills can work. As with any life skill, we only become adept with lots of practice. Some of us have been practicing for a long time, so the skill is already developed. Some will find the skill foreign as they have not practiced it much. If you want to master the skill, it will take focus and continued attention.

Develop the Ability to Sense Into One's Body (Not Letting the Mind Overrule)—This skill requires deep attention into our bodies and our energetic system. Imagine that our energy system is a large bubble three feet in all directions around us. As an exercise, approach another person and stand within a few feet of them. Your energy bubbles overlap, and there is an interaction between the bubbles. This skill is to be aware of that interaction in yourself. Try this exercise and ask yourself: Where did I feel this in my body? Did my Chakras change? If so, how? Did I modify my energy field in response? Was the interaction safe?

Note: These interactions constantly happen in our lives and can be at a much greater distance than a couple feet.

Develop the Internal Witness (Witness While Allowing Things to Be as They Are)—This skill allows us to see ourselves almost as if we are watching from outside ourselves yet sensing what is happening within. One way to train this skill is to visualize your awareness as a small version of oneself seated at the back of your brain. Imagine that you can see all the images that the eyes see, feel what the body feels, and watch the thoughts that go through the mind. From this position, your awareness can be both the observer and the doer. It takes a bit of practice, but it can be quite interesting and informative to witness ourselves as we navigate the world.

Develop Energy Skills and Utilize Energy Tools—Developing energy skills and knowing how to use them can make life much more enjoyable. As our understanding of our energetic self deepens and our skill with shifting and balancing energy grows, our field improves, and we will feel more empowered and less buffeted by the turbulent world around us. First, we need to have a deeper understanding of our energetic makeup. We strive to provide information in our work, and there are many sources of good information available. Next, we need to learn how to shift our energy in response to the environment. This skill goes hand in hand with the first skill regarding sensing into our body. When we sense other energies that we are uncomfortable with, we can shift our energies to counter and diffuse the situation. Learning this skill takes practice, and there are good teachers available if one searches.

Recognize and Disempower the Internal Judge—As we work with these skills and develop deeper energy awareness, it is important that we recognize and disempower our Internal Judge! Disempowering the Internal Judge requires lovingly accepting ourselves as we are and knowing that we are capable of change. This harsh judge wants things to be different and often states "I should have," "I'm stupid," "I am not enough or good enough," etc. When we are aware of any harsh thoughts, self-compassion and self-love support in disempowering that Internal Judge.

Expression Self-Assessment

The following questionnaire was given to participants to provide insights into which of the security expressions tend to be most active in their lives.[2] This is a short questionnaire, so the results will depend on how accurately we can self-assess. Some answers may not feel right—just go with your intuition. **Keep in mind that we all use each of the expressions, and there is no expression that is more valuable than the others.** No self-judgment is needed!

Use a separate piece of paper to record your answer or circle the **one** that most describes you. Don't *think* of what the answer should be, just **give your first response**. Do not choose more than one answer. (Trust your first thought or knowing.)

When I feel questioned, *the person questioning me* is more likely to:

1. Overthink what is happening.
2. Take care of me.

---

2 This questionnaire is inspired by Wilhelm Reich and Barbara Brennan original works. It has been adapted by various providers over the years, and this is AHA's adaptation, which we have found supports the frequency of our work.

3. Placate me.

4. Make fun of or tease me.

5. Compete with me.

In a situation where I feel judged; I tend to:

1. Disassociate.

2. Want attention.

3. Push my energy to control.

4. Be embarrassed or have guilt.

5. Reserve and hold back my energy.

Which unhealthy statement do you most resonate with?

1. The world does not feel safe.

2. If I need to ask, they don't care; if I don't ask, I won't receive.

3. I need to be right, or I'll be angry.

4. If angry, I'm embarrassed; if I concede, I'll be embarrassed.

5. There is no right answer.

The persona I project most closely matches the following:

1. I'll leave you before you leave me.

2. I don't need help.

3. I'm always right.

4. I'll devalue myself before you devalue me.

5. I have everything under control.

When not aligned with my authentic self:

1. Neither of us exist.

2. Care for me.

3. I want you to do what I want.

4. I will do things to annoy and aggravate you.

5. I won't express my love for you.

Which statement best expresses my Core Essence:

1. I am embodied.
2. I am complete.
3. I can compromise and surrender.
4. I am love.
5. What is Core Essence?

What challenges me most:

1. To exist.
2. Indifference or inaction.
3. I am not enough.
4. I gave myself away.
5. Being instead of doing.

My tendency is to:

1. Be overstimulated.
2. Want connection.
3. Not trust.
4. Care too much.
5. Push others away.

In connection with others:

1. I tend to pull away.
2. I'll ask for something, and when I receive it, it still won't feel like enough.
3. It has to be done my way or I cannot trust you.
4. I want to feel needed.
5. My way is right.

I most need to:

1. Strengthen grounding.
2. Recognize and own my needs and be independent.
3. Trust others.

4. Assert my own needs.

5. Connect to emotions and be more grounded.

I describe myself physically as:

1. Elongated, possible right and left imbalance, cool hands, feet, and core.

2. Thin, depleted, and undercharged.

3. Top heavy, warrior physique.

4. Full body, pushes forward.

5. Stiff body, less fluid movement.

My energetic security expression is:

1. Withdraws back into the spirit world, beside myself, easily overstimulated, difficulty with being grounded, prefers time alone vs in crowds.

2. Draws energy from others, speaks softly so someone must lean in to hear me, low energy, over-intellectualizes.

3. Wants to be in control, pushes others away to feel safe, feels stuck in a fight response.

4. Takes on other people's energy easily, difficulty expressing self and taking action or claiming my own space.

5. Pushes others away, doesn't allow people to really see authentic self, difficulty trusting others.

How I use my Chakras is:

1. Upper Chakras (safer to **not** be grounded) feel more spiritual-ly connected and can escape to the ethers.

2. 7th—Crown (grasping for connection to Source), 6th—Brow (to draw others in), 2nd—Sacral, lower abdomen (give myself away).

3. 7th—Crown (overuse through pushing others away), 6th—Brow (mental hook: I "know it all"), back of 4th—Heart, mid-back (overused—pushing self forward to stay in control).

4. Front Chakras (easier to connect and blend or rescue others with an open heart), 3rd—Solar Plexus, stomach area (allow others to grasp me so I can nurture them).

5. Back Chakras—all of the back of the body (easier to push energy), 6th—Brow (willpower).

Total the number of 1, 2, 3, 4, and 5 responses on the preceding questions:

1. _____

2. _____

3. _____

4. _____

5. _____

Your totals identify your predominant expressions, as follows:

1. Etheric/Withdrawing Expression

2. Empathic/Needy Expression

3. Engaged/Controlling Expression

4. Kind-Hearted/Encompassing Expression

5. Achiever/Perfectionist Expression

Notice which are your strongest or primary expressions. Going forward, we will be exploring all the energetic security expressions and focusing on experiencing the *gifts* of each expression in this book. To follow, we address each of the expressions, and specifically focus on the ways in which they show up, including:

- Energetic Security Habit
- Energy Expression
- Tools to Support Self-Balance
- Gifts
- How to Support This Expression Move Out of Habit

1. Etheric/Withdrawing Expression

Energetic Security Habit

This expression is responding to a base level fear of not being safe on the planet. In the extreme, it is a deep fear of existing. Some of the expression's responses to being unsafe include the following:

- **Leaves body:** This may seem strange, yet it is an all-too-common response to unsafe situations. When experiencing trauma, many of us energetically vacate our bodies. Some aspects of ourselves leave. We have witnessed this many times in groups—when someone suddenly feels unsafe, those aspects of self suddenly fly right out of the body. When we leave the body, our ability to fully sense the environment and even remember events is diminished.

- **Withdraws back into the spirit world to escape real or perceived dangers:** Partially inhabiting the body provides distance from the feeling of danger and allows us to cope with the feelings of being overwhelmed. When we withdraw to the spirit world, we are not fully present to others around us and may not be attentive enough to our physical body. This lack of presence dulls our relationships and may result in physical problems due to not nurturing our bodies.

- **Uses intellect as a coping skill:** This expression may use the security of the mind and intellect as refuge. If we just think instead of feel, it appears less threatening. This expression type may become very intellectual and spend most of the time engaged in ideas and thoughts and may be seen as aloof by others.

- **"Standing beside oneself":** When withdrawing from the body, some choose to keep their energy close but not actually within the body. That familiar saying, "I feel beside myself today," may well be the voicing of this energetic expression. We have noticed that energetic expression in some agitated people. The aura or energetic body is to the side or behind the physical structure rather than around it.

- **Easily overstimulated:** This expression is often very sensitive and hypervigilant because just existing is unsafe. They may be on guard in all situations and can be easily startled or stimulated by the energetic expressions of those around them. All that stimulation can lead to being overwhelmed.

- **Prefers time alone vs crowds:** If you are very sensitive and hypervigilant, crowds are a form of torture. This expression will also often have very large energy fields as a way of sensing the environment. Imagine being in a large crowd and picking up information about everyone within 20 feet of you. That is exhausting and overwhelming. The peacefulness of solitude is far more inviting and a better choice.

Energy Expression

Look for these energetic expressions:

- **Diffuse energy bubble:** This expression often has a large and diffuse aura or energy bubble. Usually the larger the bubble, the more diffuse. The energy bubble is part of our sensory system. The lack of security and need for vigilance leads this expression to expand the bubble. The diffuse nature of the bubble may increase sensitivity; however, it also means that the edges, or boundaries, are also diffuse and essentially not there. The diffuse boundaries offer an unwanted invitation for others to invade their personal space.

- **Upper Chakras are strongest:** The tendency to use intellect as a coping skill keeps the energetic focus on mind. Intellect and spiritual matters are favored, leaving less attention and energy for the lower and more physically related Chakras.

- **Connected to Spirit:** Spirit world is a place to escape and feel safer. Rather than fully embodying this incarnation, this type is only partially committed, preferring the spirit realm over the physical. They are often more psychically connected and get spiritual information.

- **Hara can disconnect from the earth plane:** Hara is in the dimension of intention. It was created by our intention to incarnate on this planet at this time. Ambivalence and fear about being here can disrupt and weaken the intentionality of Hara. In extreme cases, the Hara can disconnect from the planet. Long-term disconnection will shorten our stay on earth.

- **Can access and experience collective or unitive essence yet can be fearful of individuated Core Essence:** This expression type has strong spiritual world connections and can tap into information in the universal collective. They may be more aware than most of the interconnectivity of all human beings. Yet in spite of this expansive universal awareness, the resistance to fully experiencing this incarnation hinders the experience of their own individuated Core Essence and Soul.

Tools to Support Self-Balance

- **Strengthen boundaries and outer field:** Making changes to the habit of running a large, porous field with poor boundaries takes dedicated work. The first step is awareness. Most people with this expression have not developed the previously mentioned skill of sensing their own body. Therefore they have almost no awareness of their fields and boundaries. Once they are made aware and can begin to sense their own energy, they can quickly learn that they can control how their energy is expressed. We often teach people this awareness using hula hoops, having the participants learn to reduce the size of their field to the size of the hoop they stand in. They can also exper- iment with changing the texture or boundary of their field. Another good way to learn energetic boundaries is to attentively walk in public places while consciously shifting the size of the field and strength of the field boundaries.

- **Open eyes and keep open:** This expression type likes to close their eyes, especially when learning energy and healing tech- niques. They feel that they get more information with their eyes closed and are closer to the psychic and spiritual information. This is partly true; however, it limits the flow of information and keeps them focused in the upper Chakras. To access the full range of energetic information, we need to be well grounded and balanced in our entire energy system. Focusing on being grounded with eyes open will expand the available information we can access.

- **Bend your knees to invite self into your body:** Sometimes this expression will keep a rigid, tall, and straight posture. Bending the knees and softening the stance can allow better flow of energy and easier connection to grounding.

- **Bring your awareness to the top of your head and slowly come down into your body:** The preferred state is connection to Spirit and the upper Chakras, so start at that comfort zone. Bring awareness to the connection to Spirit above and slowly invite that awareness to descend into the body. Go slow and be aware of the sensations as awareness comes deeper into the physical. Continue down through the entire body and down into the earth. Continue down at least to the 10th Chakra about 18 inches below the feet.

- **Grounding to Pure Timeless Earth Template:** Deep grounding into the Pure Timeless Earth Template can make a difference. We have noticed this simple change can make a tremendous difference for the highly sensitive people who prefer this expression. Previously when they attempted to ground into the core of the planet, they sensed the collective distortions to the earth's energy currently enveloping humanity. This felt unsafe and they refused to connect. The Pure Timeless Earth Template does not hold those distortions and is a very safe and comforting place to connect.

- **Feel strength in the physical world (strengthen 10th and 1st Chakras):** This expression needs to shift preference from upper Chakras to a more fully balanced energetic expression. We strengthen our muscles by exercising and using them. Similarly, we strengthen our lower Chakras by exercising and using them. Regular focus on our lower Chakras, beginning with 10th and Root, is important. We can use our intention to strengthen and clear the 10th Chakra and use the 10th to energize the Chakras above. Some of our healing protocols use this concept to clear and charge the Chakras, especially the first, second, and third.

- **Encourage greater connection to your own Core Essence anchored into their body:** A characteristic of this expression is low awareness of Core Essence and resistance to full embodiment of this incarnation. Practice awareness of Core Essence and Soul. Use meditations and affirmations to encourage Soul and Core Essence to move deeper into the physical. Affirm that you embrace this incarnation.

- **Repeat to own self or others, *"I am secure, I am present"*:** Affirmations are powerful and effective. Some think it is a version of faking it until you make it. If you repeat it enough times, you eventually can believe it and be secure.

Gifts

- **Intellectual:** This security expression has a preference for the intellect, which is a wonderful gift. We need great thinkers and intellectual giants. Humanity's upward spiral toward self-realization is fed by philosophers and intellectuals using reason over emotion. Many of our inventions and the comforts in this world are designed by those of strong intellect. Our great writers help us to understand our existence on the planet and explain the existence of the spiritual realm.

- **Spiritual:** This expression type enjoys many psychic and spiritual gifts. These people are often the most sensitive, intuitive, and able to communicate with the spirit realm. The veil between earth and spirit world is thin for this expression. They are often gifted healers, psychics, clairvoyants, mediums, and channels.

- **Creative:** This expression is also very creative. They are not as easily constrained by earthly "shoulds" and are able to think expansively and freely. The mixture of spiritual and intellect is a vast source of creativity.

- **Joyful:** The frequency of the spirit realm is filled with joy. This expression loves to embrace that feeling of joy and share it with others.

- **Sensitive:** This type can be highly sensitive to the energetic expressions of others. They are able to read people's energy and intuitively "know" what is happening to others around them. Used wisely, this gift allows them to appropriately respond to the needs of others and reach out to help others before they ask. They will be quickly alerted to changes in their environment, allowing them to respond, adapt, and be resilient.

- **Light and playful:** This type can be very playful people. They can share that childlike joy and lightness that comes with the spiritual connections. They are creative in their play and like to bring others along with them.

How to Support This Expression Move Out of Habit

- **Hold your grounding first for self and then them:** This type tends to be ungrounded, living in the upper Chakras and ready to leave at the slightest threat. It is important not to leave them. Check and hold your ground. Connecting down into the Pure Timeless Earth Template will strengthen your ground and provide a more appealing grounding source to them. Next, energetically invite them to be grounded. Your being grounded offers security, and they will begin to resonate with your solid frequency.

- **Hold your outer energy bubble strong:** Model a strong aura or energy bubble. Consciously expand your bubble, yet keep firm and invite boundaries.

- **Raise your frequency to meet them where they have escaped to and slowly reground yourself, which helps them to ground:** If they are out of their body, you must meet them where they are and invite them back to their own body. As they return to their body, double check your own ground, and again envision them grounding into the Pure Timeless Earth Template.

- **Expand your Core Essence:** Core Essence is an expression of pure love. Expand your essence to embrace them and look to them to see them as pure Core Essence. They are sensitive and will know at a deep and comforting level that you see them as their spiritual self.

2. Empathic/Needy Expression

Energetic Security Habit

This expression is responding to a base level fear of not having enough and not being able to self-nurture. They look outside themselves to have their needs met. When not in expression, they may be self-sufficient, but when stressed or unsafe, they don't realize that they have the internal resources they need, so they reach out to have their needs met by others. Some of the expression responses to being unsafe include the following.

- **Sucks energy, generally from another person's 3rd Chakra to be filled:** Unable to self-satisfy, they look to others to nurture them. This includes energetic feeding. They have poor boundaries and will often hook into the energy system of others to feed themselves. This depletion they feel is rooted in their own 3rd Chakra and will often target the 3rd Chakra of others to satisfy their need to be energetically fed. This of course would be described as draining by the person who is unconsciously feeding them.

- **Speak softly so you have to lean in to hear:** This is a subtle, unconscious habit used to control those around them. When in conversation, they have a tendency to soften their voice to the point that the other person needs to lean in closer to hear them speak. As they draw you in, they also will energetically try to attach so they can feed on your energy.

- **Use their eyes to plead with you:** Through years of practice, they have mastered the "sad puppy" look. Those pleading eyes are another well-honed tactic to draw you in.

Energy Expression

Look for these energetic expressions:

- **Undercharged energy field:** They may have a deep sense of not being enough or having enough, so their energy field matches that belief and looks depleted. They may be able to charge up their field but have difficulty holding the energy over time. The fields have weak boundaries as they are looking to blend into the field of others to energetically get their needs met. Backside field and Chakras are weak.

- **Weak, sometimes diffuse Hara:** The Hara internal and external structure is weak and may be poorly defined. The Hara can be strengthened if they practice skills to support self-balance.

- **Low energy—wants someone else to energetically "feed" them:** They may feel perpetually low on energy, hoping someone else will come to the rescue and fill them up.

- **Overly verbal and high intellectual activity:** They may use verbal and intellectual skills to attract others around them. They can be smooth talkers or constant talkers. Talking keeps other people near them, providing them with the energetic nourishment they crave.

- **Develops strong connection with others in order to fill unmet needs:** Others are a major source of energy for this expression, so they have developed strong interpersonal skills in order to keep others nearby. They want to be surrounded by friends and family to have a readily available source of energetic support.

Tools to Support Self-Balance

The following tools are very useful to be able to step out of expression. Learning these tools can minimize the undesirable aspects of the expression and enhance the gifts of the expression.

- **Learn to nurture oneself to find nourishment in one's life:** Coming to the realization that you can nurture yourself is important. Look for small ways to start where you can self-satisfy and notice that you can get what you need without it being given by others. The little steps can lead to bigger steps as one realizes that life itself can be nourishing if we are in balance and harmony.

- **Bend knees and ground to the Pure Timeless Earth Grids:** The earth is a source of energy and support. There are a myriad of techniques to ground and connect to the earth. Creating habits and rituals to regularly connect with our planet and draw energetic nourishment is one way to build towards self-nurturing.

- **Align Hara to support and save oneself to stand on "own two feet" to allow for Source connection and flow:** Hara work is important as a means to connect to both the earth and our Divine source. Hara is our energetic backbone and central column of strength. As we focus on clearing and strengthening Hara, we will be able to hold and sustain personal energy.

- **Allow energy fields and Chakras to come into open, balanced flow:** Once a stronger Hara is achieved, focusing on our Chakras and the associated fields will be easier. There are many resources available to help strengthen our Chakra system. Guided meditations, reading, or energy practitioners can be useful to get our Chakras and fields cleared and balanced. Once balance is achieved, the goal should be to work toward the ability to self-regulate and self-sustain.

- **Nurture love and compassion for SELF:** This expression is very externally focused, so shifting to internal focus and self-love can be difficult but not insurmountable. It takes a concerted effort to shift the focus and learn to trust and love oneself. There are many books and resources available to help make this shift. It will be a long but rewarding journey to self-love.

- **Repeat *"I am whole"*:** Affirmations are powerful and effective. Keep repeating this affirmation until you can believe it. You are whole!

Gifts

- **Kind, compassionate:** This expression can be very kind and compassionate. Their outward focus makes them attentive to the needs and experiences of others. They will go out of their way to show kindness and compassion to others struggling with the little and big situations in life.

- **Giving:** This expression enjoys giving, seeing the joy that giving creates. Part of the expression was created by not having enough. The deeper that need is satisfied, the more generous they will become in gift giving.

- **Caring, nurturing, loving:** They thrive on having others around them. Their focus on others can be very caring and nurturing, showering people with their love. The more they are able to self-generate energy, the more they will give to others in this caring manner.

- **Intelligent:** These people tend to express intelligence and mental acuity. Their 3rd Chakra focus activates the mental field. They like ideas and mentally stimulating activities.

- **Articulate:** They are verbally confident and articulate in getting what they want. They are also good at expressing their mental processing and will excel at using language to engage others. They will show their caring compassionate side in words as well as deeds.

- **Generous and supportive:** This expression can be very generous in time and energy to support those around them. They will hang around to support you and be there as your friend.

- **Tend to focus on being rather than doing:** Doing things together is less important than just being with others. They can also be content to be with themselves and their mental processes when their needs are met.

- **Emotionally intelligent:** These people will tend to have high EQs. Their focus on others as part of the expression has taught them great skills for understanding and working with a wide range of human needs and types.

How to Support This Expression Move Out of Habit

- **Hold your own ground first:** This type will want to tap into you, so it is important to be able to hold your own and model standing on your own two feet. Connecting down into the Pure Timeless Earth Template will strengthen your ground.

- **Turn your body at a slight angle so that they can't energetically hook into your 3rd Chakra:** Their natural tendency is to connect with your 3rd Chakra, so turning slightly away makes it harder for them to do so.

- **Have your field more structured (1, 3, 5, 7, 9):** Their fields are generally less structured, so it is important to model a healthy field structure for them. Rather than offering them energy, we offer them a model of what they can do for themselves.

- **Expand Core Essence to allow them to feel nurtured by being the Divinity so they can experience their own Core Essence:** They want to be nurtured and cared for. Meeting them with Core Essence feeds them at a deeper level than if they were drawing energy through your 3rd Chakra. Stay in the highest frequencies, offering them a chance to resonate with that frequency and get in touch with their own Core Essence.

3. Engaged/Controlling Expression

Energetic Security Habit

The wounding here was about trust in others. When they needed help, no one was there for them. They learned to fend for themselves, so they are always alert for threats. They may also harbor a deep fear of being bad or hurting others. Some of the expression responses to being unsafe include the following.

- **Display of power or will, often as energy over the back of their head like a cobra attacking:** This expression holds a strong energy, especially in the upper body. When challenged, they may send their energy field arching over the person they are interacting with, holding them in this grasp of energy as they try to control or bend them to their will.

- **Energetically tries to control others:** This expression resists being controlled. The perfect defense against control is to control others first. They use their strong energy, will, charisma, and intellect to maintain control of others. They want to be right and position themselves to win.

- **Pushes away so as to not be betrayed:** The strong energy expression is effective to keep others away and maintain strong independence. They are guarded about their energy, not wanting to allow others in.

- **Feel stuck in a fight response:** This expression repeatedly found short-term relief by standing up for themselves, but it is not an effective long-term strategy. The expression of standing up, ready to be strong and defending, keeps them in a perpetual state of readiness. Flight or freeze isn't a response for them, so they are always ready to fight.

- **Not trusting the individuality of others' Core Essences:** Their deep-rooted distrust of their own Core Essence manifests as a distrust of all others. At a deep level, they understand that they are powerful, and power misused can be dangerous. They don't want to be dangerous, but they project that danger and distrust onto others.

Energy Expression

Look for these energetic expressions:

- **The back side of Chakras are strongest:** This expression characteristically holds considerable power on the back side of the Chakras. They can bring that back side power over themselves in a defensive interaction.

- **Structured upper body:** They typically have larger upper body and torso. They are often physically strong, so the upper body is well muscled. This physical structure holds a similarly structured energetic body.

- **Strong Hara but wants to control others:** This expression will have a well-structured and strong Hara. They may hold a wider Hara and project their strength through that strong Hara.

- **Weak legs and not grounded:** They may have thinner, weaker legs supporting that strong upper body. They prefer the upper

Chakras and have not developed strong grounding practices to maintain the lower body Chakras and grounding to the planet.

- **Strong Core Essence:** Their Core Essence comes through strongly. They may have deeper connections to their essence and interests in spirituality.

Tools to Support Self-Balance

- **Trust self and others:** To balance and heal this expression, they need to develop deeper trust and love of self. That love and trust of self will be mirrored in interactions with others. Trusting others will come from that deeper trust of self.

- **Create balanced energy field:** This expression's tendency is to have a strong back side of the Chakras. Bringing conscious awareness to a balanced energy field will be supportive. As the field becomes more balanced, the defense of bringing energy over the back will diminish.

- **Surrender to being present and human:** To realize that one is not in control of most things is to recognize our humanity. When fully present and observing rather than doing, we can realize that very few things are under our full control. This self-realization is balancing and regulates the activation of this expression's need to control.

- **Infuse and regulate Hara to trust:** This expression already has a strong Hara. Learning to infuse the Hara with love and using the power of the Hara for good creates more self-trust and trust in the goodness and Divinity of others.

- **Meet another as equally Divine, sensing their Core Essence:** This expression has an innate awareness of their Core Essence but is not so good at seeing that within others. Conscious efforts to see others as Core Essence and meeting them in that space melts all distrust and any need to be defensive.

- **Repeat *"I am secure, I am light"*:** Affirmations are powerful and effective. Keep repeating this affirmation until you can believe it, for you are light.

Gifts

- **Leader:** This expression naturally rises to leadership positions. They are seen by others as very confident and holding the right attributes of a leader. In expression, they will want to dominate others, but when in healthy balance, they will be very effective leaders.

- **Strong, competent:** They are often physically strong and like physical activities that strengthen the body and showcase that asset. They tend to excel at physical activity and will be confident and competent.

- **Resourceful:** They are intellectually fluid and creative, able to come up with resourceful answers to problem situations. They are good problem solvers.

- **Strong integrity:** This expression has a strong sense of integrity and moral compass. They keep their word and expect others to reciprocate.

- **Big heart full of love:** When balanced and in their pure essence, they like themselves and others. They are responsive to others and share their love with all those around them.

- **Big energy, charismatic:** This expression tends to have a big field and takes up a lot of space. They can be very charming and charismatic. This skill was honed while in expression to get their way, however, in a balanced state, these are wonderful gifts.

- **Confident in one's own power, able to empower others:** They are very confident and want to share that confidence with others. They empower others and cheer them on, fully believing everyone can be as confident and effective as they are.

- **Self-reliant, competent, and able to think clearly in crisis:** When in crisis, they do not leave or quit or wait for others. They take command and keep their wits about them, thinking through the best approaches to the situation.

How to Support This Expression Move Out of Habit

- **Bring your awareness to how you are holding your energy field:** Regulate the size of your field to a normal arm's distance from your body and evenly balance your energy, front and back. This will support them in staying more present and to establish a deeper trust in others.

- **Bend knees and ground to the Pure Timeless Earth and invite your energy into the earth:** This expression may want to push your energy or come up over you, so you need to be firmly planted. Connecting down into the Pure Timeless Earth Template will strengthen your ground to hold your own without being threatening.

- **Soften your field with a non-threatening stance:** Open your palms to them, lower your shoulders, and soften your body. Make sure your posture is relaxed.

- **Break eye contact with them so they can let themselves back off from "fight mode":** Focus your gaze below their face, giving them time to soften and realize you come in peace.

- **Expand Core Essence and gently meet them:** They may be able to sense their Core Essences and Divinity, yet they still see others as a threat. Meeting them with Core Essence slowly and gently will allow them space to recognize that you are not a threat and can meet at Core Essence level as equals. Stay in the highest frequencies, offering them a chance to resonate with that frequency and meet you, Core Essence to Core Essence.

4. Kind-Hearted/Encompassing Expression

Energetic Security Habit

This expression has wounding related to their will, freedom, and unique sense of self being stifled or denied. They get stuck in that space, not fully able to act and recognize themselves as completely separate selves. They simply endure the situation. Some of the expression responses to being unsafe include the following.

- **Merge or encompass others:** We are all energetically connected to each other, yet we are individuated forms. This expression has trouble understanding their fully individuated form and energetically encompasses others with their energy. They may have trouble differentiating themselves from others as they blur the boundaries. Others are often unaware of, yet at a deeper level uncomfortable with, that violation of boundaries.

- **Porous field:** They often have poorly defined field boundaries. Their fields are porous and amorphous. They don't clearly structure their fields to mark where they end and others begin.

- **They take on other people's energy easily:** Their porous fields and low awareness of boundaries lead them to take on others' energy easily. They readily experience the emotions and thoughts of others near them. Low awareness leads them to internalize those feelings, not being able to separate the energy of self from others. This can be confusing as they feel the emotions yet may not know what the origin is.

- **Large energy field:** This expression may run very large energy fields as they are not self-contained. The large field increases their sensitivity and diminishes the protective nature of the fields.

- **Boundary domination:** They may have poor boundary practices. Their big, porous fields interact with the fields of others around them. They will unknowingly merge or transgress other people's boundaries. This lack of boundaries will flow into other aspects of life, not knowing when to get involved in (or stay out of) other people's affairs.

- **Can be prickly:** Their inner frustration can show up in a passive-aggressive style. When this occurs, their fields will become prickly while outwardly they are acting nicely.

- **Difficulty expressing self, taking action, claiming own space:** This expression's hurt makes it difficult for them to stand up for themselves. The expression has them enduring the situation, so acting out and claiming their own identity is difficult. They have internalized the social messages of "You are not worthy," and so have trouble accepting their self-worth and claiming their own space.

Energy Expression

Look for these energetic expressions:

- **Unstructured levels 1, 3, 5, 7, 9:** Normally these layers of the aura are seen as structured lines and grids. This expression tends to have less structure in these layers. The 1st layer can often be thick and dense rather than a thin, well-defined layer. The fields are amorphous so as to easily flow and take on the energy of others. This may show up physically as a less structured, softer body type.

- **Stronger energy in lower body:** They tend to hold their energy and push down, resulting in more energy flow in the lower part of the body and Chakras. They may ground well.

- **Strong Heart Chakra:** Their Heart Chakra is often open, and they express energy outward from the heart. They use their heart to communicate and connect to others.

- **Hara needs clarity towards good boundaries:** The Hara may be large, but it is not as strongly defined in this expression.

Tools to Support Self-Balance

- **Begin to be assertive:** This expression has habituated a lack of assertiveness, so they need to give themselves permission to step forward and be assertive. The world can be safer to be more assertive now, so test it and experiment instead of always being accommodating.

- **Become more open spiritually:** Explore your spiritual nature and develop practices and expressions that allow you to tap into your true self as Core Essence.

- **Find the structured levels of the energy field to support in creating balanced boundaries:** This expression tends to have low awareness of boundaries and does not realize how big they can be. Exercises that create awareness of the overall size and the ability to balance by shifting size and structure are especially beneficial for this expression. With practice, you can learn to change the size, porosity, and structure of the fields as a whole and individual layers. These exercises will anchor in the sense of self-autonomy and help in developing healthy boundaries.

- **Invite Hara to create the structure in the field:** Hara work will be useful for creating deeper structure within the Hara. The structure and definition within Hara will aid in creating more structure within the auric fields as well.

- **Tap into Core Essence as the Source of knowing you are full and whole:** Deeper connection with Core Essence will help to understand the wonderful, powerful self you are as an individuated spirit. That realization can then flow into accepting that you are worthy and valued as an individual human and are free to express that.

- **Repeat *"I am sovereign"*:** Affirmations are powerful and effective. Keep repeating this affirmation until you can believe it—then you will be sovereign.

Gifts

- **Loves others:** This expression has a big heart, always thinking of others and sharing their love with people. They can be joyous and delightful people.

- **Helper:** They are always helpful and thoughtful, often offering to help before asked. They have always been outwardly focused, so they have learned to anticipate the needs of others.

- **Deeply grounded strength:** This expression has practiced sending energy down, so they ground easily and hold this grounded strength.

- **Stamina and strength:** They have honed the art of being steadfast. They may have a tremendous ability to keep going when others are tired. Their stamina and strength show in physical tasks as well as mental and emotional duties.

- **Patient:** They have learned to be patient and can be there as long as needed. They are not as driven by clocks and expectation as much as other energetic expressions are.

- **Creative:** They can be very creative in their ideas as well as artistic expression. 2nd Chakra is creative as well as connection to others. They love to express themselves through this Chakra.

- **Enjoys silence and stillness:** They love other people, yet they don't require stimulation as much as others. They can be quite content to spend time in silence and stillness. When they are in this expression, silence and solitude are a refuge from the over-stimulation of their large fields.

- **A large capacity for energy:** They can hold and share a large amount of energy. They typically have big fields. When they have learned to regulate and create healthy boundaries, that large field can be filled with love and support for others.

How to Support This Expression Move Out of Habit

- **Hold strong yet soft boundaries:** Start from a place of being centered, grounded, and anchored into the Pure Timeless Earth with your Hara. Bring attention to your own aura and boundaries. Balance your aura and hold it at a size that allows you to have boundaries that are clear yet soft and affirming. Set the intention that you are welcoming, but they are not allowed to merge with you.

- **Stand to the side, not directly facing them to honor not taking or needing anything from them:** Shift your posture and positioning to be slightly off to the side or turned to the side. If we come in directly, it triggers their desire to take care of us.

- **Gently expand Core Essence to meet them:** Focus on your own Core Essence. Slowly and gently expand your Core Essence to meet them at Core Essence, honoring them as individuals.

- **Regulate your field to theirs without "needing" anything from them:** Allow their field to acclimate to yours and regulate your field to match them in size. Just "BE" with them.

5. Achiever/Perfectionist Expression

Energetic Security Habit

This expression is focused on adhering to rules and the correct or best ways for all things. They are hypercritical of themselves and others, wanting to be perfect. Some of the expression responses to being unsafe include the following.

- **Pushing away:** Energetically, they like to create a security barrier around themselves, pushing out in all directions with their energy. It is more like a force field than a protective bubble.

- **Verbal knives:** They see things as more "black and white." If they don't like something or someone's behavior, they will comment without regard to sensitivity. Their words can feel like knives. Although they may not be consciously choosing to cut with their words, they can cause deep damage.

- **Porcupine:** When challenged, their normal outward pushing of energy can become even more forceful and bristling like a porcupine. Energetically, they are telling you to keep your distance.

- **Not allowing people to really see their authentic self:** Their constant pushing out of energy prevents any closer examination and entry by others. They know they are not perfect and don't want you to find that out either.

- **"I am my performance":** They judge themselves by their performance and how close they are to perfection. They will also judge you based on how you measure up in your performance.

- **Emphasis on correctness, so much that they may miss out on the beauty of life:** They tend to focus on how things are not perfect. They would focus on asymmetry rather than symmetry. They are looking for flaws more than beauty. This has useful qualities but takes pleasure out of life.

- **Difficulty trusting others:** Rarely do others meet their high standards, so others are not to be trusted. If they want something done right, they do it themselves. These expressions make it difficult to trust and work with others.

Energy Expression

Look for these energetic expressions:

- **Structured grids 1, 3, 5, 7, 9:** These levels of the human aura are present as lines and grids. This expression is the most structured of all expressions. The gridwork in these layers of the field is well-defined and solid.

- **Disconnected from the second and fourth levels of their field (emotions):** The second and fourth layers of the human aura are fluid and move with the emotional and heart energies of the system. Although these layers are present, this expression is not connected to these layers and their emotional energy. They may have little awareness of this information and the state of these layers.

- **Strong Hara:** The Hara of this expression can be strong and rigid, especially in the lower portion of the Hara.

- **Can be disconnected from Core Essence and don't believe Core Essence exists:** Their Hara is strong but primarily connected to the earth. Their spiritual connections to Core Essence may be restricted. They tend to be more focused on religious correctness rather than the mystical spiritual realms.

Tools to Support Self-Balance

- **Regulate Hara to feel emotions to support the energy system:** This expression has a strong Hara, but it's not fully balanced and supportive. They are well-connected below, but less above. Focusing on balancing above and below is helpful. There may be Hara damage in the mid-Chakras that could use attention and repair. Bringing attention to the flow of energy rather than holding strength will support overall balance.

- **Strengthen Core Essence and Soul/Oversoul connection:** Strengthening the connection to Core Essence and Oversoul needs to start with shifting and affirming the belief system regarding our spiritual nature. Reading, discussion, and validation may be needed to make the shift. Once the belief system has shifted, it will be easier to make a deeper connection, which will aid in balancing the Hara.

- **Balance structured and unstructured fields:** The structured fields tend to be over-structured or rigid, so softening these fields will be beneficial. The unstructured fields of the second, fourth, and sixth are less developed and could flow more to create balance. Creating deeper awareness of the flow of emotions, love, and subtle energies would be supportive.

- **Nurture and return to Core Essence often:** Finding daily practices that bring attention to Core Essence and our spiritual nature will foster that missing connection with Spirit.

- **Allow love to flow with ease to and from others:** Sensitivity here is usually low, so it will take some training. Practice allowing love to flow. Start with simple exercises with people close to you. Visualize connecting at the heart and giving permission to allow love to flow in and out of your heart. As the sensitivity increases, practice with others and at a distance.

- **Repeat *"I am authentic"*:** Affirmations are powerful and effective. Keep repeating this affirmation until you can believe it—you are authentic!

Gifts

- **Dependable:** People preferring this expression are punctual, dependable, and do things the right way. They take pride in doing everything well, if not perfectly. If they say they will do it, they will come through for you.

- **Achiever, high will:** They excel at most things they do. They have a strong will and determination to do things right. They are measuring themselves by their performance and they don't want to disappoint.

- **Perceptive and respectful of boundaries:** They are firm about personal boundaries, holding a rigid structure themselves. They expect you to stay clear of their boundaries and will also respect yours. They can be quite perceptive as they are constantly analyzing the world for compliance with their perceived set of rules. They will notice anything that does not fit the rules.

- **Structured:** They are highly structured and rigid about things. They expect a certain order and tend to develop deep expressions. Spontaneity disrupts the expected expressions and is not welcomed. They are happier if everything happens as expected.

- **Passionate:** They can be very passionate about the things or causes they believe in. They will dive in headfirst and work hard to make the object of their passion the best it can be.

- **Organized:** This expression can be very organized, sometimes to the point of obsession. One of their mottos is: "A place for everything and everything in its place." They bring this same view of organization to companies and businesses. They can be very good at finding the most efficient and effective way to organize work and make processes flow.

- **Good at saving and budgeting:** Attention to details and organization is a gift when dealing with financial matters. Sticking to the rules and avoiding spontaneous decisions is helpful to keeping finances in good order. You can be sure the bookkeeping aspect of their work will also be well organized and all accounts will be balanced.

- **Great at reasoning and solving problems:** This expression makes good engineers. The expression has trained them to notice how things work and what flaws look like. They are able to find ways to improve anything, constantly looking for the best approach or ways to make things better. They are good thinkers, able to reason through complex problems and find good solutions.

How to Support This Expression Move Out of Habit

- **Hold your ground first for self:** This expression can be strong and want to push you away, so you need to be firmly planted. Connecting down into the Pure Timeless Earth Template will strengthen your ground to hold your own.

- **Soften your field so you are less threatening:** They will sense that shift and be more open to you.

- **Stand in a state of love and compassion:** From a place of being grounded and centered, set your intention to be love. Radiate love and compassion for them. All judgment drops away when we are pure love. They will sense that acceptance of them as they are, and the need to be perfect will diminish.

- **Expand Core Essence to meet them to allow them to sense their own Core Essence/Divinity:** They usually do not sense their Core Essences and Divinity, so they may have little experience with this sensation. Meeting them with Core Essence models what they may feel and meets them as an equal. Stay in the highest frequencies, offering them a chance to resonate with that frequency and get in touch with their own Core Essence.

Experiencing the Awareness of the Different Types of Expressions and Supportive Action to Move Out of Habitual Expressions

In the workshop, we used group exercises as a tool to experience the energetic expressions of each type and practice supportive actions when each habit was displayed. The exercises were very informative for the participants as they gave actual body awareness of the expressions and their responses, allowing the learning to integrate at a deeper level.

This group exercise was designed to allow everybody to experience the security expressions in two ways. One way was that they were instructed to project the expression. We all have some level of understanding of each expression, so when instructed, they were able to energetically create the desired security expression by intent. The second half of the experience was to interact with someone projecting a particular expression. This gave them an energetic confirmation of how that expression feels. When they experienced that expression, they were instructed to shift their energy into the healthy/healing response and notice how the interaction changed. When they shifted their energetic response away from the conditioned expression response to the healthy supportive response, the person projecting a certain security expression also shifted as they no longer felt unsafe. Most people in the group were able to identify the expressions and hold a supportive healing response.

These exercises are only the beginning. To become competent at these responses on an everyday level, it would take a considerable amount of conscious awareness and practice. Perhaps the best way to experience and learn about the energetic expressions is to pick one or two study partners and work together. Learn about each other's expressions by sharing the results of the questionnaire. Then practice the supportive action or response, especially when the predominant expressions are presenting themselves. It is easy to do when the expressions are more dormant. When the expression is triggered, the energy is expressed more forcefully, and it will be more difficult to stay in the supportive role. It may be too easy at first to slip into your programmed expression response if they trigger you. Keep practicing, and you will get more proficient. If you have a difficult interpersonal relationship with an individual that would not be a willing study partner, find a friend and willing partner that has similar predominant security expressions. Learn with your friend, and it should help your other, more difficult relationship.

Chapter Eighteen

Clearing Soul Contracts and Styles of Connection

We presented soul contracts as a possible framework to help us understand our purpose and help explain the meaning of our life interactions. Our friends that do intuitive and psychic work tell us that the most common question their clients ask is: What is my purpose?

These are common questions that linger for most of us, also phrased as: Why am I here? What is my mission? Some people have big, important tasks with major impacts on society. Most people have smaller roles to play. We are all contributing to the collective evolution, but most of us are working through soul lessons focused on our personal growth and awareness, which is how we are contributing. The following perspective on soul planning and soul contracts may clarify our life situations. It helps us move out of shame, blame, and victim thinking and into the realization that we are actively involved in this planning process. It also helps to put some of the harsher aspects of life into perspective.

Soul Growth and Contracts

It is a privilege to be here on earth and for our soul to experience this plane of existence. It is an exciting time to be on earth as we move through this accelerating period of soul and earth evolution and ascension. Messages from many psychics indicate that earth school is one of the harder schools, and we have earned this opportunity for greater soul growth on the planet.

We are here to experience contrast. Earth is a place of dualities and diversity. We need to have these contrasts to understand and learn the differences in our values and experiences. We need to experience the highs as well as the lows. To understand deep love, we also need to experience the absence of love. We need to experience abundance as well as scarcity. So with each lesson, we gain empathy and understanding by experiencing both sides of the duality.

We chose the plan. Our true essence is much more than what presents itself on earth. The higher aspects of our being (Soul, Oversoul, and Core Essence) are all involved in the planning process of our incarnation. We work with our spiritual guides and pure Source to develop an outline for our time on earth. We decide what important lessons will be the focus and how we can best experience these lessons. We create agreements and contracts with other souls in order to learn these lessons. These plans and contracts get woven into the matrix of our Incarnation Grid and Soul Field Grid to guide and direct our journey in this lifetime. Free will allows us to fluidly make changes in the plan, which may affect the learning process.

We choose our family and friends. Prior to our incarnation, we decide what family will best support our lesson plan and choose the supporting cast of friends that will help us. We come up with a loosely scripted lesson plan that gets refined along the way as we learn and continue to make choices. Soul contracts are agreements with other souls to help each other with our lessons. We need to have the contrast—if we need to experience abandonment, then we need to contract with another soul to have that experience. In this perspective, the soul agreeing to abandon us does it out of service, not from malice. They may also need to experience the other side as they abandon us. We make many contracts, both for our personal lessons and to be in service of others as they learn their own lessons.

Soul contracts can span multiple lives. It is not uncommon to have soul contracts that continue between multiple lifetimes. Some contracts may be set up that way at the start. Some contracts may persist until we learn the lessons. We may need to experience the same situations many times before we finally learn our lessons. We all have parts of life where learning seems to come quickly, and other parts of life where learning is extremely difficult. When we keep making the same mistake again and again, it is a sign that this is a deep expression and probably a soul lesson. These are the things that can take many lifetimes to learn.

Experiencing gifts and challenges of the expressions is all part of the learning process. Our souls will have the opportunity to experience each of the energetic security expressions multiple times as we learn and evolve. Understanding the expressions and realizing that they are only energetic expressions and not the actual person or soul is helpful. If we can learn to recognize the expressions and responses, we deepen our understanding and empathy of others. That deeper understanding facilitates our soul growth and learning.

How we view and experience the world depends on the clarity of our filters. We see and experience the world through our cloudy filters, missing the true reality of what is before us. That distortion affects our ability to correctly see and learn our lessons. The deeper that distortion, the more we are likely to see life events as something happening to us, rather than something happening for us, or with us. When we can clear our filters of distortion, we are able to see more clearly that life unfolds for us and in support of our soul contracts and plans. Our lessons become easier when these distortions are removed.

Clearing Soul Contracts and Soul Field Grid Experiential

Our soul contracts and agreements are woven into the matrix of our Soul Field Grid. Through the exercise of our free will and decisions made through distortions in our filters, our current set of agreements may be out of alignment with our highest good. Unhealthy choices and associations can follow us through multiple lifetimes. This experiential is designed to release that which does not serve and realign our contracts with the highest good and evolution of our soul.

This exercise was done in pairs during the workshop. As you read this book, we suggest that you find a willing partner to share the experience of this exercise in order to get the full benefit and meaning. We also encourage discussion with your partner and journaling about your insights. The exercise was done with the receiver/client sitting in a chair, although it may allow more relaxation and depth if done on a treatment table.

We invited the person acting as practitioner to align with Source, then ground and connect to the Pure Timeless Earth Template. A quick expansion through the Advanced High Frequency Shift technique would be perfect as preparation. The receiver was invited to just relax, receive, and be willing to release all that does not serve them. Once the practitioner was prepared, they placed one hand on the front side of the High Heart/Soul Seat of the client. The other hand was placed on the backside of High Heart. From this position, the practitioner asks the guides to join in and do the work of transmuting, releasing, and realignment of any unhealthy, complete, or unneeded soul contracts or agreements. The guides will use their special filters or tools as needed. The practitioner is instructed to stand in support and just BE. Just to stay present and BE the space, the conduit of love, allowing for the release to occur.

The first step is to ask the guides to help retrieve any aspects of the soul the client may have given away. We all do this throughout life, in difficult situations, when we submit to others, or go against our plan. In doing so, we allow others to hold a piece of our soul. This is not helpful to us or the one holding that aspect of us. This step is a form of soul retrieval. Allow time for this energetic exchange to happen.

The second step is to ask the client to release any aspect of the soul of others that they may be holding. We ask that those soul aspects be returned to their rightful sacred home. We sometimes hold aspects of another to be kind and unburden them. It is not helping us to hold onto others this way. This step is often surprising to many clients. Most people understand the first step and realize they have given away aspects of themselves. They seldom realize the extent to which they are holding onto the soul aspects of others. Often the energetic shift of this release is felt by both the client and practitioner. Allow time for this to complete.

The third step is to ask that all contracts that are complete or no longer in the highest good of the client be dissolved and released. This step dissolves agreements that were made for the wrong reasons or through distorted views and relationships. Allow time for this to complete.

The fourth step is to ask that only loving contracts or agreements are allowed to flow in all directions. This reinforces the previous step and assures that contracts in place and yet to be made are in the service of love. This includes contracts for the client's lessons as well as contracts where they are serving the lessons of other souls. Allow time for this to complete.

When complete, the practitioner releases their hands from the client. The practitioner may then hold the feet or shoulders of the client, visualizing the client grounded and connected to the earth. They step back and consciously release their energy from the client. The practitioner can invite a discussion with the client to hear their experience and share anything the practitioner sensed. Giving the client a chance to journal is recommended.

Repeat the exercise again with your partner, trading the roles of client and practitioner.

Styles of Connection

These styles of connection are present in all relationships. They are part of the dynamics of family life, our interactions with friends, and even found in our professional and business interactions. We all strive to communicate and get along with the others in our life. We want people to like us and to share friendship, love, and connection. We all want to be heard, seen, and respected. We each have our own personality, preferences, and energetic expressions. We each have personal preferences in how we like to give and receive love—how we connect with others.

For this segment of our work, we were originally inspired by Gary Chapman's book *The 5 Love Languages: The Secret to Love that Lasts* and his work on this topic. However, it was when we aligned it with our high frequency work that we really came to understand everything within the framework of energetic connection. Understanding the energetics of connection is a simple and effective way to strengthen our interactions with others, enabling us to experience more joy and harmony in all our relationships. When we understand the different styles of connection, we can begin to see how others prefer to connect.

A common misconception is to assume others have the same preferences that we do when it comes to connecting. We often show our affection and connection in the same style that we would like to receive. Along the lines of what Chapman taught in his book, thinking of these styles as different languages is helpful. If we expressed our connection in English and the receiver only knew Spanish, the receiver would not fully understand our intent. Similarly, if we express our connection in a style that the receiver does not prefer, they may not see it as an attempt at connection. This mismatch of connection languages can cause relationship friction. When we don't see connection the way we expect it, we often don't recognize it. We can feel ignored in the midst of a shower of affection if it comes in an unexpected language.

The secret is learning the style preferences of others so we can connect in a style they understand and embrace. When we understand these styles better, we may also be able to recognize when someone is trying to demonstrate their desire for connection in a style that doesn't resonate with us. If you can recognize that effort, you can then appreciate that they are trying to express that desire. This can bring you closer and deepen your relationships. Expressing our intention to others in a style that matches their expectations can shift them out of unhealthy energetic security expressions and open them to more meaningful interactions.

Gifts of the Heart

Perhaps you prefer to show connection through gifts and presents. These are often small tokens of your attention, although occasionally they are bigger items. For you, these physical gifts symbolize your intentions, much like the exchange of rings at a wedding are symbolic of the bonds of love. You are good at finding simple, heartwarming symbols of your relationship or objects that remind people of fond memories. These gifts may not require any money at all to give. You have a unique ability to visually symbolize interpersonal relationships in an object. It is good to keep in mind that not everyone will appreciate the gifts in the manner you give them. Others may miss the symbolism and find the gifts shallow or superficial. When sharing your gifts, staying fully present in your heart allows you to release the need to receive back, and give truly from a place of love.

Focused Attention

If this is your style, you will feel most appreciated when you are spending focused quality time with another. You want to be seen and heard and get undivided attention. Sharing a meal together, dancing, taking a class together, or time together on a car ride are all meaningful moments for you. Sharing conversation, emotions, and focused time is just perfect. The context of your activity is not so important, it is the focused attention and shared moments that count. You dread situations where someone is indifferent to you or so focused on their electronic devices that you don't seem to exist. Remember—creating this focus of attention with another requires a centered mind and present heart while staying grounded to support the flow of energy.

Validating Language

For some, the preferred style of connection is through affirmation. If this is you, you most appreciate receiving validation through words. You enjoy compliments, praise, cheerleading, encouragement, and any expression of support and admiration. For you, words speak louder than actions. You appreciate those that can verbally communicate well. You are also probably more sensitive to harsh and critical words. Criticism may feel like a knife, cutting deeply. When connecting in this way, it is important that we are truthful with our words, holding their powerful intention and genuine emotions. Before speaking, feel yourself grounded and in alignment with energetic truth. Speak clearly, communicating your intent.

Deeds of Endearment

Demonstrating your affection with thoughtful gestures and deeds could be your preference. You may prefer to show your intention for connection by cooking a meal, cleaning the house, running an errand, or some other act of service. For you, talk is cheap—actions speak louder than words. This can be a constructive way to make relation-ships work. It can be a joy rather than a chore to do something for those close to you. If this is your preference, it is important to be mindful of your role and not be trapped into doing all the dirty work without receiving reciprocal connection. When you demonstrate your intention to connect in this manner, be mindful of anchoring your Hara to the Pure Timeless Earth to be fully grounded and present in your actions.

Kinesthetic Attention

If this is your preference you want to receive connection through physical contact. You are a great hugger and want to show your intention to connect with some form of touch, a hug, a pat on the back, maybe just a hand on their shoulder. If the others are not reciprocating, just being physically close may feel good. For your romantic con-nections, it will be kissing and more touch. Kinesthetic connection can be an impactful way to show devotion and fondness. This style can be connected to our family upbringing, and some social settings may discourage physical touch. If this is your style, you have probably learned when and where it is safe to express yourself in this style. Honoring another's energetic boundaries supports safe space, allowing for a grounded heartfelt connection.

What Is Your Style Exercise

We conducted an exercise to encourage the participants to ponder these styles and think about the styles of those people close to them. We suggest you take out your journal and do this yourself.

- Pick out four or five people such as family, friends, coworkers, and influential people in your life.
- Add yourself to the bottom of your list.
- For each person on the list, write down their name and the top two styles of connection preferences for that person. To do this, ask yourself: How do they like to be shown or receive connection?
- Think about your style preferences. How do you most often express your connection? What is your favorite way to receive connection? Write down your top two style preferences.

- Then look at your list to see where your styles overlap with the others on the list. Think about how often you express your attention and connection in ways that match the style of the others on your list.
- To take it further, can you identify times when they are reaching to connect in ways you don't recognize?

You can repeat this exercise as many times as you like if you find it helpful to better understand and enhance your relationships.

Chapter Nineteen

Trauma Dissolution and Planetary Alignment

This section covers the protocol that was developed to help transmute some of the trauma we all carry and prepare ourselves to better assist in bringing in the frequencies necessary for planetary alignment. We are all connected in the beautiful web of creation on this earth. All personal healing becomes group healing as we collectively support and help each other transform.

Stress-Trauma Link

Holistic practitioners have long known the link between stress and disease. Medical research in recent years has been confirming that link, detailing the myriad of ways in which stress undermines our ability to stay balanced and healthy. Some years back, when focusing on autoimmune work, angelic guides were communicating that all of the autoimmune diseases were just different manifestations of the one root cause: stress. Guidance was suggesting that the mental churning associated with stress results in a breakdown of our organs. That breakdown in the organ system reduces the organs' effectiveness at properly cleaning and clearing out toxins in the body. Over time, the reduced efficiency results in a buildup of waste and subsequent dysregulation of our physical system.

We all have stress. There is no such thing as a stress-free life. As humans, we have a tendency to want to organize and control aspects of our life and create plans for our future. Life is messy, so our organization gets disturbed, and plans change. All of that creates some level of stress. Some of us are more resilient than others. One of the keys is to make decisions about the stressors and move on. If we don't decide, then at some level we keep churning, which creates more stress. When we don't relieve the stress, it gets stored as little energetic bubbles somewhere in our being.

Some stressors are small and are just the everyday irritants that generally don't add up for most people. Medium-size stressors are the bigger bumps in the road of life such as job changes, relationship changes, new life coming, important people leaving, as well as accidents and other big changes. These medium stressors can add up, especially when we experience multiple stressors simultaneously. Medium stressors are more likely to get stored as energetic bubbles in our being. If we don't find a strategy to relieve this stress, it can build and start to degrade our health, sending us into a downward spiral.

Big stressors are more difficult to manage. They are the traumas of life such as being a victim of assault, long-term abuse, war, accident trauma, perceived deep wrongs, and loss of very close relationships. Since they are hard to manage, some people try to just stuff them away and bury them. Unfortunately, the body remembers, and it just silently churns, creating more stress and storing more energetic bubbles. Some people are able to face the challenge, learn, forgive, grow in self-love, and heal.

This work is just one of many aspects of healing trauma and disease processes. Ultimately, to be successful at handling all stress, we need to find productive ways to deal with and release the trauma and stress, reduce the churning, learn ways to be more self-compassionate, and love ourselves deeply.

A key part of the protocol here is to release the emotional bubbles of energy that are buried in our organs, our fascia, and the multidimensional aspects of our beings. The release is usually not at a conscious level and does not involve reliving the memories of the trauma and stressors.

Aiding Planetary Alignment

We believe that this work is a mix of personal and planetary healing. All planetary healing begins at an individual level. We can all be part of the movement to help in the evolution and ascension of human consciousness. This planetary acceleration requires a shift to higher frequency energies and thoughts. If we can shift our frequency on a personal level, we can become a conduit to allow higher frequencies to come through to the earth and all of humanity. We think it is similar to the idea of a radio relay station.

When we can resonate at the higher frequencies, the frequencies flow through us, relayed into this space and time. We have many helpers on a galactic scale that are assisting to raise the collective frequency. Our task is to purify ourselves to be the best possible relay station. We can do this by clearing and transmuting all layers of our being, aligning, and entraining with the highest frequencies at each matrix level. As we clear ourselves, we can surrender to service of the highest good. Maintaining the higher frequency allows us to play a small role in the grand plan to change the planet.

Trauma Dissolution and Planetary Alignment Experiential

We created this experiential healing exercise to provide the participants with an opportunity to release and transmute trauma stored within their being and deepen their grounding and connections to our planet. This exercise was done as an energy healing trade. Participants paired up. One assumed the role of the practitioner, the other the role of client or recipient of the work. After the session was complete and time was taken for discussion and reflection, the participants reversed roles so that both had an opportunity to give and receive. We recommend finding a willing partner to experience this protocol both as a receiver and a practitioner.

The purpose of this technique is to:

- Transmute layers of stored trauma and stress within the client's body
- Provide balance and reverse dysregulation of trauma in the client's body
- Clear trauma throughout multidimensional aspects of client
- Purify client to be a clearer receiver of planetary alignment frequencies
- Align client with Pure Timeless Earth Template

- Integrate pure frequencies through all levels of matrices from planetary to Divine levels

Step 1: High Frequency Shift—Self/Practitioner

The first step of the session is Advanced High Frequency Shift (AHFS) for the practitioner. This is done while holding the feet of the client. The AHFS brings the practitioner to the optimum elevated frequency to be the conduit for the client. It also serves to entrain the client in that elevated frequency, beginning the process of healing.

Step 2: High Frequency Shift—Client

The next step is to perform the client version of the AHFS, ensuring the client is also at an elevated frequency.

Step 3: Self-Love Infusion

The unique part of the protocol begins with the practitioner moving to the right side of the treatment table. The practitioner slides their left hand under the sheets, from above the shoulder, down to the back side of High Heart. The right hand is placed on the front side of the client's High Heart. Begin visualizing the holding of both front and back aspects of High Heart. Invite in the swirling, Divine masculine frequencies of white-gold. Allow those frequencies to blend and permeate High Heart.

Next, invite in the swirling, Divine feminine frequencies of rose-gold. Allow those frequencies to permeate High Heart and blend with the white-gold frequencies.

Next, bring in the frequencies of pure, Divine gold. These are the frequencies of Source, the one. Allow these pure love frequencies to permeate High Heart and blend with the white-gold and rose-gold frequencies, creating a triangle, the trinity.

Connect the seat of their soul with High Heart. Ask their soul to show you their true self, their Divine Essence, a projection of pure, unconditional love. Invite them to accept and absorb this feeling of pure love. Knowing that this is who they really are!

Invite them to allow these frequencies of love to flow into their expressions of energetic boundary responses. Ask them to embrace the following affirmations:

- Affirm you can hold safe personal boundaries
- Affirm that you can resist the reactionary response to energetic projections of others
- Affirm that you can respond in loving and appropriate manner to the energetic projections of others

Allow these frequencies of love to flow into and activate each of your styles of connection, allowing you to fully give love, inwardly to yourself first, then outwardly to others. Ask them to embrace the following affirmations:

- Affirm your deep self-love and love of others
- Be of service to yourself and others
- Allow yourself to receive gifts
- Make quality time for yourself and others
- Allow yourself to receive loving physical connection

Step 4: Charging Sequence

The charging sequence opens and balances the energetic body while raising the frequency of the entire energy system. It reinforces the crystalline grid system, providing greater stability in the physical form. At each position, the practitioner will visualize a swirl of rainbow iridescent and effervescent light that flows from each hand. The intention, that the swirling light dissolves and lifts trauma stored in the body and surrounding fields and grids, as crystalline structure is set.

The practitioner starts by moving to the foot of the table. Placing one hand on the bottom of each of the client's feet and allowing that swirl of rainbow iridescent and effervescent light frequency to begin flowing. Allow that energy to flood into their body, transmuting as it goes. At each hand position, practitioners will be visualizing the creation of two triangles. One triangle points down, with a line connecting their hands and lines connecting to the apex at the 10th Chakra (approximately where they are currently standing). The other triangle points up, lines connecting the hands and lines towards the apex at the 8th Chakra. Each position is held, allowing time for the dissolution of trauma, alignment of the energy, and formation of the triangular grids.

Charging Sequence Steps: The following are the hand positions.

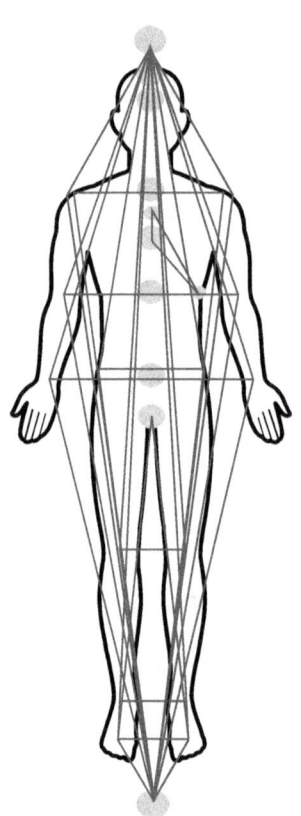

- Solar plexus reflex points of feet—creating triangles to the 8th and 10th Chakras.

- Same position, now connect to the Root Chakra and the 10th Chakra.

- Both ankles—creating triangles to the 8th and 10th Chakras.

- Both knees—creating triangles to the 8th and 10th Chakras.

- Both hips—creating triangles to the 8th and 10th Chakras.

- Both wrists—creating triangles to the 8th and 10th Chakras.

- Both elbows—creating triangles to the 8th and 10th Chakras.

- Hands on the Spleen and Thymus, mentally connect to the Heart Chakra, creating a triangle of the three points.

- Both shoulders—creating triangles to the 8th and 10th Chakras.

- Position right middle finger on the Brow Chakra, position left middle finger on the Zeal Chakra (at center indent point on occipital ridge). Position both thumbs on the Crown Chakra. Visualize a triangle connecting these three points, activating the head centers.

Step 5: Charging and Integrating the Earth Star/10th Chakra

Next, move back to the foot of the table. Visualize the client's Hara connected to the true, pure essence of the Pure Timeless Earth's core. Through the Hara, visualize the client's Earth Crystal within the core of the Pure Timeless Earth and their 10th Chakra connected to the Earth's core energy. Allow time to integrate with the pure earth's core energy. Visualize generating a sphere from the Earth Star/10th Chakra energy six to eight inches in diameter at the 10th Chakra. As the sphere builds, ask that transgenerational trauma be dissolved.

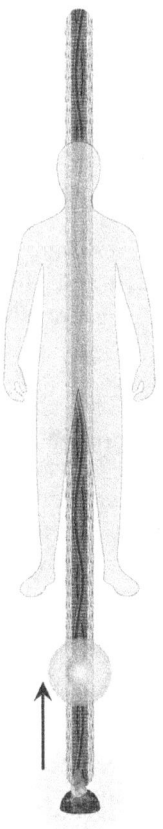

Step 6: Clearing the Mirrors and Integrating the Earth Star/10th Chakra

With the assistance of the guides, move your hands up to Root Chakra, allowing this glowing sphere to migrate up through the Hara. Integrate the charged 10th Chakra energy with the root, clearing the first mirror, the reflection of the projection of self. Allow time as needed for integration.

With the assistance of the guides, move your hands up to Sacral Chakra, allowing this glowing sphere to migrate up through the Hara. Integrate the charged 10th Chakra energy with the sacral, clearing the second mirror, the reflection of what should be. Allow time as needed for integration.

With the assistance of the guides, allow this glowing sphere to migrate up through the Hara.

Integrate the charged 10th Chakra energy with the Solar Plexus Chakra, clearing the third mirror, the reflection of our hidden gifts. Allow time as needed for integration.

With the assistance of the guides, allow this glowing sphere to migrate up through the Hara.

Integrate the charged 10th Chakra energy with the Heart Chakra, clearing the fourth mirror, the reflection of compulsions. Allow time as needed for integration.

With the assistance of the guides, allow this glowing sphere to migrate up through the Hara.

Integrate the charged 10th Chakra energy with the Throat Chakra, clearing the fifth mirror, the reflection of the Divine union. Allow time as needed for integration.

With the assistance of the guides, allow this glowing sphere to migrate up through the

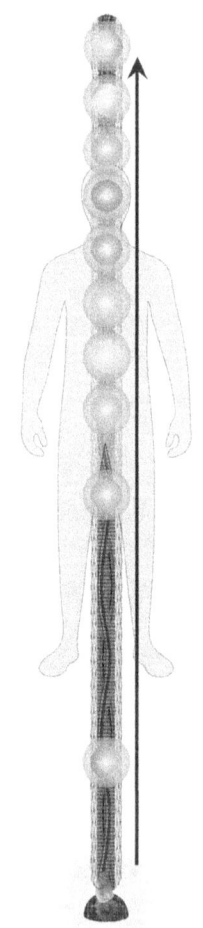

Hara, stopping at each of the upper Chakras, allowing time as needed to integrate at each Chakra before moving up. Integrate the charged 10th Chakra energy to the Brow Chakra, Crown Chakra, 8th Chakra and 9th/Soul Star Chakra. When this step is complete, pause to sense the deep integration and notice any shifts in the client's energy system.

Step 7: Expanding the Heart Chakra Torus

Next, move to the right side of the table and shift your focus to the client's Heart Chakra and heart field.

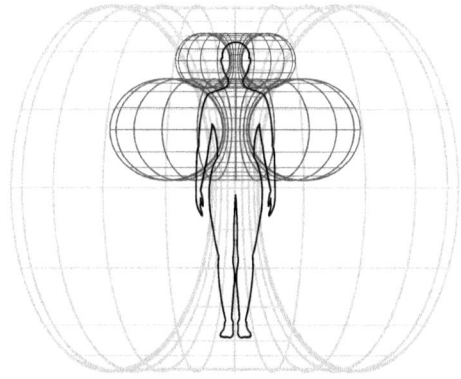

Visualize the heart torus created by the Heart Chakra's energy.

Using your hands, invite the torus to expand.

Start below the heart, sweeping upwards, out, and around, tracing the heart torus.

Repeat this sweeping motion five or more times, each time starting lower, sweeping higher and out as the torus expands.

Continue until you are sweeping from below the 10th Chakra up to the 9th Chakra.

Then hold your hands to the side of the client, allowing the torus to stabilize at that expanded state.

Step 8: Filling the Expanded Heart Torus with the 12 Rays

Stand along the right side of the table. Place your left hand on High Heart and your right hand on or above the Heart Chakra. Pause and connect deeply at their Heart and Soul level. Call upon the 12 Rays of Light and their supporting Study of Divine Light. Ask the guides to provide what is needed for the highest good of this beautiful soul. Be present as the guides fill the expanded heart torus with the needed frequency, tones, and vibrations. Hold until this feels complete.

Step 9: Lightbody Holographic Activation

Move your hands so that your left hand slides under the client behind the Heart Chakra. The right hand returns to the position on or above the Heart Chakra. Settle in and attune with the zero point of Heart Chakra. Let the zero point open and expand into a vast space.

Connect with the client's multidimensional Oversoul. Ask that their Lightbody be recalibrated to the highest frequencies of self-love and Divine Mind they can integrate at this time. Hold as the holographic Lightbody template is recalibrated.

Step 10: Clearing and Transmuting the Grids

The next step is to clear and align the grid systems with the purified and transmuted Lightbody.

The guides will provide a set of filters to clear and align the grid system. The filters may appear as four concentric hoops.

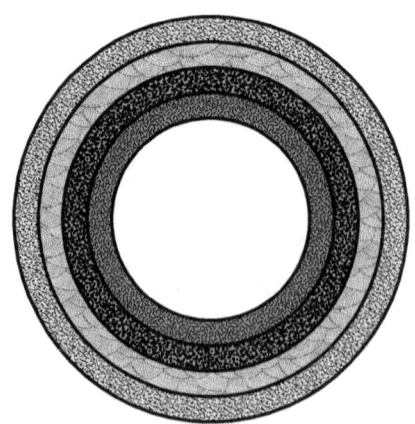

Visualize holding these large hoops. Starting above the 9th Chakra, very slowly draw the hoops down the body and past the 10th Chakra.

As you draw the hoops through the gridwork, the guides are

assisting. The filters align and clear the Incarnation, Soul, Fascial, and DNA grids.

After passing the 10th Chakra, let go of the first set of filters, remaining at the foot of the table, the guides will provide a second set of filters, This set of filters may appear as a concentric set of five hoops. These filters will transmute any non-beneficial energies and inserts.

Visualize holding the hoops. Starting below the 10th Chakra, very slowly pull the hoops up the client's body, past the 9th Chakra. These filters align and clear the physical, emotional, mental, spiritual, and holographic Lightbody matrices.

Allow the energy of the charged 10th Chakra to fill any transmuted inserts with the highest frequencies of light and love through all Chakras.

After passing the 9th Chakra, let go of the set of filters and come back to the foot of the table.

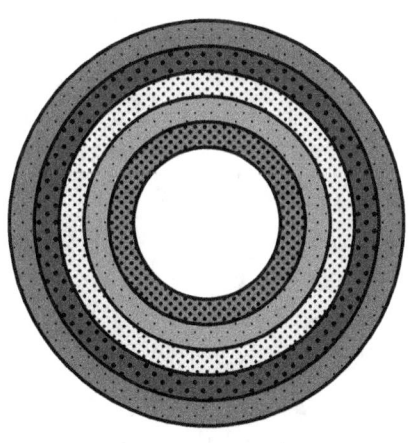

Hold your hands at the point of the 10th Chakra. Invite the energy of plasma and the comet beings to come through your hands. Visualize the comet beings zipping through interdimensional space up the body as they transmute all that does not serve the client. They transmute at cellular, subatomic, and extradimensional scales. Allow the flow of plasma and comet beings to slowly swirl up the client until it has cleared through the 9th Chakra.

Step 11: Alignment with the Pure Timeless Earth

Continue standing at the foot of the table, shifting your focus to align the client with the highest frequencies of the Pure Timeless Earth core. The focus here is on the client's energy, although your blended energy will also follow and become one. Imagine the perfected Pure Timeless Template of earth. Align with the pure core of the timeless planet. Allow a deep connection into the zero point of the earth's core. Allow your essences to blend and entrain with the earth grids. Experience becoming one with the inner matrix of the earth. Sense the group collective weave together into the earth core matrix.

Step 12: Alignment with Earth Core, Land and Seas, Protective Fields, and Grids

Continue standing at the foot of the table, shifting your focus from the earth core and expanding your awareness. Attune and align with the land, mountains, forests, prairies, and deserts. Invite the elders, guardians, and ascension angels to assist. Feel the land align with the Pure Timeless Earth core matrix.

Bring awareness to the very tip of your client's breastbone where the Elemental Heart Point is accessed. Invite the frequencies of the time-less earth and connection to the elemental consciousness to flow up and connect to the point (at this point we go to the Quantum).

Allow for alignment and activation. This activation connects them with the Timeless Elemental Consciousness for greater communion with the earth keepers.

Continue expanding your awareness. Attune and align with the frequency of the oceans and seas. Invite in the dolphins and whales and mammals of the sea. Sense the oceans and align with the Pure Timeless Earth core matrix.

Move awareness out to earth orbit. Invite ascension angels and guard-ians. Attune and align with the timeless planetary gridwork, fields, and matrix. Sense that earth's outer matrix aligns with the Pure Timeless Earth core matrix and our collective woven into the matrix.

Step 13: Letting the Energy Flow Through Into the Earth

Just go into surrender mode. Sense and allow every aspect to know this state of being.

Be aware of the frequency that flows through now; know it as love. Feel immense gratitude from Beings at all levels, being thankful for this gift. Reflect back gratitude and love. Hold here until you sense a culmination of all the frequencies flowing with and through you and the client as the energy comes to a still point.

Step 14: Zipping up the Field

Next step is "zipping up the field." This is done by holding the palms of both hands on the soles of the client's feet. The practitioner holds each position for about 10–15 seconds, allowing the energy to flow with the intention of sealing in the work. Work your way up the body, "zipping" in the sequence shown in the next graphic.

1. Hands on bottom of feet.
2. Left ankle and right knee.
3. Right ankle and left knee.
4. Left knee and right hip.
5. Right knee and left hip.
6. Both hips.
7. Left wrist and right elbow.
8. Right wrist and left elbow.
9. Left elbow and right shoulder.
10. Right elbow and left shoulder.
11. Both shoulders.
12. Left shoulder and right side of the head.
13. Right shoulder and left side of the head.
14. Both sides of the head.

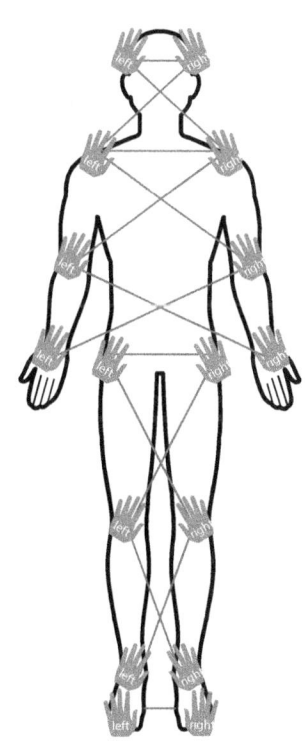

Step 15: Completion

As a finalizing step, the practitioner visualizes streamers of gossamer threads woven and infused with iridescent diamonds, swirling around and creating a three-inch-thick cocoon of energy. Starting at the Soul Star, allow the gossamer thread to swirl around, filling all bodies and fields around the client. This protects and holds the energy, allowing time to integrate and assimilate the gifts of the session.

Chapter Twenty

Weaving It All Together

This chapter weaves together the concepts covered in the workshop. Our expressions as a human in this lifetime are the result of an amazing number of factors all coming together. There is far more purpose to our lives and interactions than we tend to think. Our souls were guided to make many choices and contracts for this appearance.

Your soul chooses a location, family, friends, personality, and physical appearance for this grand experiment. When we think about the care that has gone into making us just who we are, we should be immensely grateful and joyful for our situation and realize the depth of love that pervades all those around us. Unfortunately, in the earth-bound world, where we have forgotten most of that, it is a bit hard to stay positive about the situations that life keeps bringing us. By our thoughts, actions, deeds, and soul planning, we attract situations/ people into our lives for our soul lessons. People and situations can be used as the mirrors to see ourselves and our challenges. This can be a challenging concept for some to accept, but it is one way in which we are able to fulfill our sacred contracts and improve at a soul level to find our way back to the Divine Mind of Love.

This section seeks to weave together how the various ways we present ourselves fit our energetic expression—these expressions have served us well and become habits as we navigate experiences in this life, learning our lessons. The Chakras are part of our energetic structure and serve as sensory centers and messaging centers, filtering our energetic interactions with the world and others. Our thought patterns and personal interactions influence and are mediated by our Chakra system. We all practice each of the variations of the energetic security expressions. The energetic security expressions are how we react and present ourselves to all these people we have attracted into our lives. The mirrors are equivalent to the *Golden Rule*: Do unto others as you'd have them do unto you. The styles of connection are equivalent to the *Platinum Rule*: Do unto others as they would want done unto them. We know how to use all of the styles to express our connection, although we tend to favor a few.

Here we link those preferred expressions, styles, mirrors, and Chakras as an attempt to bring more conscious awareness to our behaviors so that we may enjoy the gifts of our expressions more often and show love to those around us in ways they recognize and prefer.

1st Chakra—Etheric/Withdrawing Expression

We think this expression is most associated with the first or Root Chakra, which is located at the pelvic floor. This is our basic primal survival Chakra (tribal). It is instinctual and about our physical health and presence on the planet. It holds keys to our unconscious beliefs about deserving physical life and well-being, and it regulates the physical system and flow of universal energy.

The first mirror reflects the projection of self, and it mirrors the present moment by showing us what we are currently energetically expressing to the people around us. Often when we are in error in our own beingness, it is related to Root Chakra, as it is usually a survival issue or hurt regarding the security of being on this planet. If we are present in the moment, safe and aware of our own energy, this mirror reflects happiness and security.

The style of connection most closely associated with this type is focused attention. Those with this expression feel most loved and secure when spending meaningful, focused time with their partners or with others sharing their bonds of connection.

Anchoring the gifts of the etheric/withdrawing expression into your body and energetic system requires attention to grounding and moving energy down into the lower Chakras, especially the root. Consciously working to create a sense of security and purpose on the planet will be helpful. When able to stay in presence, inviting a balanced ego, the gifts of this expression will generously reward you with the ability to embody your spiritual gifts and create joyfulness, an expanded intellectual capacity, and playful yet sensitive equal connection with others.

2nd Chakra—Kind-Hearted/Encompassing Expression

This expression is most associated with the second or Sacral Chakra, which is located just below the navel. This Chakra mediates the expression of feelings and creativeness with the world. Our connectivity to all others and our sexuality. It also supports the unconscious template of those interactions, helping us stay resilient through changes and adaptations. This expression tends to lack good boundaries, unable to create healthy connectivity with others, either taking on the other's energy or merging with them.

The second mirror is more subtle than the first mirror as it is not as overt. It is the reflection of what should be. So if situations or people trigger/cause an emotional charge, it is often where we have stored trauma or rigid belief systems. We can be the most judgmentally harsh on those who have a similar trauma to our own. We also spend considerable energy judging ourselves against perceived social norms. If we pay attention to this mirror, it shows us how to use the gifts of acceptance and understanding for ourselves and those we judge.

The style of connection most closely associated with this type is deeds of endearment. Those with this expression feel most connected to people close to them. They demonstrate their intention with thoughtful gestures, small deeds done in kindness, and acting before they are asked. The deeds of service need not be much—however small, they will be noticed and appreciated. This style will be more than happy to do things for you or take things off your plate to help ease your burdens.

Consciously working to create clear boundaries and awareness of self and others will help you stay out of the extreme of kind-hearted/ encompassing expression habits. When able to stay grounded and present and invite a balanced ego, the gifts of this expression will generously reward you with great creativeness, stamina, and strength. Others will revel in the shower of loving energy you provide.

3rd Chakra—Empathic/Needy Expression

This expression is most associated with the third or Solar Plexus Chakra, which is located at the diaphragm or solar plexus. This Chakra is the source of our self-esteem and self-power, our ability to succeed in the world, our thoughts and mental structures. It also holds our mental templates of self and reality, our understanding of how the world works. This expression often has a sense of depletion in the 3rd Chakra, always looking to others to fill that missing sense of self.

The third mirror is the reflection of our hidden gifts. We often have both a physiological and psychological response when we encounter others that retain a feature we wish we had. Or we may wish to "belong"—we wish to reclaim that aspect of ourselves through another. It is always something we can reclaim within ourselves, which is why we find it so attractive in another. We are most often unaware of the level of regret we carry for not having this feature. Once we become aware, we can move forward in deciding if it is worth attaining or not.

The style of connection through which this type prefers to receive is through physical kinesthetic attention. They want to touch and be touched to acknowledge and express connection. The physical connection can be sensual when in a partnered relationship; however, it is primarily just about being in physical proximity and can include touch, such as a hand on the shoulder or a passing touch, whether playful or showing connection.

The habits of the empathic/needy expression can invite conscious grounding and connecting with the earth. Learning to stand on your own feet is important. Through the connections with earth, Source, and deeper awareness of self, this type can learn that nourishment and affirmation can come from within rather than from others. With these realizations and by staying grounded and present, we can invite in and embody the gifts of this expression. The gifts will create a strong self-nurturing while expressing deep kindness and love for others. You will be emotionally intelligent, generous, and supportive of others and just enjoy being the wonderful soul you are.

4th Chakra—Achiever/Perfectionist Expression

This expression is most associated with the fourth or Heart Chakra, which is located at the center of the chest, near the nipple line. The Heart Chakra holds the ability to love, giving and receiving with others. Heart Chakra balances the lower and upper Chakras. It holds connection to our heart's desire, our unconscious beliefs about love, and relationships with others and the Divine. This expression can be so focused on doing, performance, and the outer manifestations of life that they can have difficulty connecting with their Core Essence, inner beauty, and the flow of love in their life.

The fourth mirror, the reflection of compulsions, presents differently than the first three. It shows us ourselves through addictions and compulsive behaviors to the point that we end up living our lives around these compulsions, becoming dependent on outer forces for perceived love. This mirror may be the hardest one to stare into and see oneself, for the most forgotten love is love of self.

This expression's preferred style of connection is to receive love through gifts of the heart, demonstrations of attention through material tokens such as gifts/presents. While they are physical forms, they are symbolic of your affection, reminding them of the relationship or friendship as a small trinket would. Some may find this form feeling shallow and superficial, yet it is about the ability to visually symbolize a relationship into a physical object to hold.

The great challenge for the achiever/perfectionist expression is to find ways to awaken, connect, and balance the emotional, spiritual, and love energies. When able to restore that forgotten love of self and stay grounded and present, they are well-positioned to enjoy the gifts of the expression. The gifts of this expression such as being dependable, passionate, organized, and a great problem solver are wonderful skills for navigating the physical world. Untroubled by the physical world, there will be plenty of time to love and be loved while releasing your innate sense of passion to achieve life's desires.

5th Chakra—Engaged/Controlling Expression

This expression is most associated with the fifth or Throat Chakra, which is located at the base of the neck. Throat Chakra is associated with expression, communication, creativity, and alignment with the will and guidance from Spirit. The Throat Chakra is also an access point for external spiritual guidance.

The fifth mirror reflects the Divine union, the expression in how we live our lives. These are often learned through our experience of growing up in the family of origin. This mirror reflects our belief system around the parental roles, masculine/feminine roles, and even the Divine masculine/feminine aspects of creation. It reflects how we align with these archetypes and what relationships we have with these as we live our lives.

This expression has a preference for validating words as a style of connection. They most appreciate receiving love in the form of language: affirming words, praise, compliments, and expressions of support or admiration. They show their connection through language as well as freely expressing that love in affirming ways backed by powerful intentions and emotions.

When the engaged/controlling expression can learn the balance of deeply trusting self and others, recognizing the inherent connection of all, the need to control diminishes and they are able to create a strong, healthy, balanced ego, and embody the gifts of the expression. Those gifts of charisma and the ability to empower others with a big heart full of love combined with strong competent leadership can make things happen to serve all.

Another Look Into the Mirror

It is time for another look into the mirror. At the end of the workshop, we asked our participants to once again gaze into their mirror. We also suggest you use a hand mirror or a bathroom mirror to look deep into yourself as you read, do, and ponder the following. Give yourself a minute or more as needed with each bullet point:

- Fill yourself with the gold frequencies, feel your **Self-Love and Compassion**.
- Remember your **Energetic Security Expressions**, knowing you can move out of expression into presence. Focus on the gifts of your most used expression.

- Feel your **Chakras & Energy System** fill with higher frequencies, and become a beacon of light.

- Know that you have positively shifted your **Physical, Mental, and Emotional Health**.

- See all of life as beautiful and a **Mirror Reflection** of Self.

- Knowing **Styles of Connection** allows you to create healthier energetic connections with others more consciously. How can you show your connection in ways that will be better received and gracefully accept connections that come in a style you may not recognize?

- You are here to complete the **Soul Contracts** that are for your highest good, releasing all others.

What do you see in the mirror now? Take a moment to record those thoughts, feelings, and sensations in your journal.

The Divinity Mirror

As we can appreciate ourselves and the way in which we understand and navigate the world, it increases our ability to understand others. Using the mirror concept, we can understand that others are mirrors of ourselves. We can realize the deep interconnectivity of all humans. When we can learn to see beyond all the masks and projections to the real essence in those around us, we can see that brilliant light that is their soul.

In those moments, that person is still the mirror, but they have now become the Divinity mirror. For that beautiful reflection you see in them is actually a reflection of your own Divinity, your shining soul. Welcome home!

Chapter Twenty-one

Closing Invocation: April 2022

We finish the workshop in ceremony, using the following invocation to reinforce the learning and help set the new frequencies as the participants return to their normal lives. The ceremony included a ritual to cement their bond as a group and commit to global service.

Clearing the Lens of Self-Understanding and Self-Compassion to Facilitate Healthy Relationships and Boundaries

I stand in the template of the Pure Timeless Earth, my awareness fused with the crystalline matrix of our planet.

I inhale, deeply connected into the powerful energy of earth, my entire being activated.

I bow in honor to the ancestors, elementals, and benevolent beings embodying and protecting this and all space. I am grateful for the ease and security I experience.

I breathe in, experiencing the new Divine frequencies of pure love. I am a vessel of unified awareness; I am the embodiment of sacred self and pure love.

I open my arms to embrace the Divine light of source. I am filled, one with Source.

I have released all limited ideas of self and reality. My heart and mind are open as I journey on to greater understanding of self and others.

I see clearly the mirrors of my existence.

I commit to clear personal boundaries and compassionate energetic interactions with others.

I am a servant of the Divine plan, embracing the highest possible frequencies and dimensions flowing through me. These frequencies purify and amplify all aspects of my Being, accelerating self and planetary ascension.

My heart rejoices in the union of the masculine and feminine aspects of the Christ Consciousness and to my Oversoul. I am awake!

Chapter Twenty-two

Creating Our Body of Work

In 2015, the triad of co-creators began meeting regularly via phone. This evolved to video conferencing twice a month, and by late 2016, we decided to create a collective work to bring forward to the public in order to share our guided joint information. In the fall of 2017, we hosted our first retreat together in Colorado Springs, Colorado.

We continued to collaborate as a collective, bringing the work forward with new material for each retreat. In time we added additional collaborators. This guided collaborative process and series of workshops has spawned a considerable collection of works.

Some of AHA's work has already been brought forward in other workshops or in print with our published books: *Embodying Higher Frequencies [2022], Awakening to Higher Frequencies [2021],* and *Everything is Energy (including you!)[2020],* which was recently translated into Spanish, *Todo es energía (¡incluso tú!)[2024].* As we progress in sharing our work, we intend for it to be the subject of additional books and/or web-based material, focusing on and embracing the following topics and concepts:

- Esoteric Healing
- The Science of Your Biofield and the Impact on Healing
- Limitlessness of Your Soul
- Expansion of Multidimensional Healing
- Advanced Back Chakra Activation
- Enhancing Your Ability to Guide Self & Others From the Heart
- Illuminating the Quantum Fascia

- Claiming Your Heart's Note/Sacred Toning and Embracing the Collective Symphony
- Core Essence Expansion and Elevation: Living as Divine, Moment to Moment
- Exploring your Extradimensional Quantum Existence
- Joyful Communion with Your Essence and the Divine Collective
- The Power of Your Heart: Embodying Esoteric Healing
- Nurture Your Intuitive Gifts
- Amplifying Your Lightbody
- Your Soul's Longing and Purpose
- Multidimensional Fascia Healing: Unwinding, Releasing, Repatterning and Realigning
- Deeper Understanding of Your Energetic Make-up
- Weaving Awe and Gratitude Into the Fabric of Life
- Igniting Your Curiosity and Dancing with the Fireflies
- Activate and Resonate with the Pure Timeless Divine Earth Template

Chapter Twenty-three

Conclusion: Final Notes

It is our wish that the work that we have shared supports the evolution of humankind by contributing to the collective of Lightworkers on planet earth and connecting to the vast consciousness of Light Beings that are ever-present for us to raise all souls to even higher frequencies.

We know that this work is one of many paths that the supporting guides use to bring in the new frequencies to earth in support of our common evolution. We hope that each of these paths merge into a clear road for humankind to find its way home.

We realize that we are but a small group that holds this high frequency of light for the collective, but we fully trust that we each make a difference in this evolution. Our intention is to build on our expanding web-based content to support the material in this book. Our hope is that expanding access and enabling all types of learners to study the material will lead to broader sharing of the highest possible frequencies.

Tim and Franny

Appendix

Glossary

Advanced High Frequency Shift (AHFS): An updated and more detailed exercise to train your energy system to access more of the highest available frequencies and prepare for the more advanced energies as our evolution continues.

Angels: Spiritual beings that act as messengers or agents of the Divine. Available to assist us when asked. It is thought we are always surrounded by angels, and each of us has one or more guardian angels.

Ascended Master: A spiritual being that was once in human form, mastered ascension, and karmically not required to incarnate. Part of the team of spiritual beings assisting humanity to evolve and ascend.

Ascension: The process of ascending to a higher spiritual level, level of enlightenment, or higher state of consciousness.

Axiatonal Grid: Axia=axis or direction; Tonal=sound or vibration; Electrical in nature, the Axiatonal Grid combines color and sound to realign blood, lymph, and the nervous system into Divine template. The Axiatonal meridian system is part of the step-down process from Lightbody to physical body. Equivalent of acupuncture meridians but connecting the Oversoul and resonant star systems with the physical. Through the Axiatonal lines, the gridwork of Lightbody is translated into programming of the human body.

Basic High Frequency Shift (BHFS): Exercise is foundational to training your energy system to access available frequencies and prepare for the more advanced energies now coming through.

Consciousness: The awareness of self and one's surroundings.

Core Essence: Your Light, the Divine spark of God that you are now, have been, and always will be. The position of Core Essence is the current expression of the frequency you are in this physical dimension. It also embodies the frequencies that reflect or represent other aspects of you.

Empath: A highly sensitive person with an ability to sense, experience, or take on the thoughts, feelings, emotions, or physical pain of those around them. Many empaths experience these sensations yet have trouble discerning the origin of the sensation.

Energetic Inserts: Energetic inserts are subtle programs inserted into our matrix or body. Think of them as like an app on your phone or computer. They can change our energy, behavior, and even our physical structure. They can be beneficial or non-beneficial. Obviously, we want to keep the beneficial ones and eliminate the non-beneficial ones. It is best to use the wisdom of the Guides when transmuting inserts.

Energy Therapy: A therapy (there are many versions) where a trained practitioner consciously works with the human energy field and energy matrix of a client to restore balance and harmony.

Extradimensional: Originating and operating outside the known physical three-dimensional physical reality. Working in many dimensions beyond the normal 3D of time and space.

Flower of Life: Sacred geometry form, at least 6,000 years old. Contains fundamental forms of time and space. We use it as protection and as a vehicle.

Frequency: In electromagnetics, it refers to the numbers of waves that pass a fixed place in a given amount of time. So it is basically the rate of vibration.

Guardians: Spiritual beings that serve a role as protector, sentinel, or defender.

Guides: Our team of Spirits (usually disincarnate) that serve to teach, guide, and protect us.

Hara: Column of energy we incarnate on. Our intentions of life purpose creates an energetic connection from Spirit to form on this planet. Hara has an internal structure and an external structure.

High Frequency: Heightened levels of energetic awareness and existence. When in a state of high frequency, the human energy system functions at a more optimum state and has greater awareness of higher levels of consciousness.

Holograph: In our 3D world, a Hologram is a projection of a light field as an interference pattern that creates a light field. That field produces an accurate reproduction of the original image such that it can be viewed from different angles and creates the illusion of a true 3D object. Our usage of the term is from the perspective of a multidimensional reality where projections into the Matrix from many dimensions creates holographic fields which carry organizing energies and can be perceived by some sensitive people.

Lightbody: A holographic projection upon the Matrix comprising many organizing fields. These fields define our spiritual and physical manifestation in this world.

Merkaba: Considered to be a Lightbody vehicle used to connect with and reach higher frequencies. It also is known to be multidimensional, allowing access to the other planes. It is used as a tool by Archangel Metatron.

Metatron's Cube: A representation of how energy flows through the Universe. It contains all Platonic Solids also holding 13 circles within. It is used as a cleansing device.

Möbius Strip: A möbius strip is a continuous surface with a twist in it. A simple example can be made by attaching the ends of a ribbon to each other with a single twist. We commonly use one that looks like a figure eight. Additional twists can be added to create more complex objects. Wires wrapped in a möbius strip can create scalar waves.

Möbius Coil: A möbius coil is a series of möbius strips that can create a continuous surface with a twist in it. Our physical structure has examples of möbius coils in our DNA at a cellular level and vascular system on a larger scale. These biological structures create scalar waves, thought to be part of the intercellular communication system.

Oversoul: The primordial or highest level of soul, where it retains both the properties of being the self as well as being the selfless one.

Quantum: Properly defined as the smallest unit of many forms of energy. At the smallest of scales of quantum physics, the rules of interaction become different from classic physics. Our use of the term refers to complex interdimensional interactions of energy at this smallest scale.

Rays or Ray of Light: A title for a specific or focused consciousness of the Creator. In this usage, light is information. Each Ray is already part of our soul waiting to emerge. The Rays are a form of teaching this information—they are a Discipline or Study of Divine Light.

Tree of Life: The tree of life is a geometric pattern or symbol used in multiple mystical traditions, generally associated with the Kabbalah. Although there are many interpretations, it usually depicts the process of moving the primordial energy of source into the physical manifestation of this creation. In the reverse direction it could symbolize the spiritual ascension of humanity

Vibration: An oscillation or movement of a fluid, elastic solid, or medium, or an electromagnetic wave.

Vivaxis ("Axis of Life"): Your own personal generator in the energy field into which you are born. Formed within a few weeks of your birth. An agreement between the Earth and the Soul that will support what you came here to do in this lifetime.

Bibliography

Bailey, Alice. *Esoteric Healing*. Lucis Publishing Company, 1953.

Brennan, Barbara Ann. *Light Emerging: The Journey of Personal Healing*. Bantam Books, 1993.

Chapman, Gary. *The 5 Love Languages: The Secret to Love that Lasts*. Northfield Publishing, 1992.

Dale, Cyndi. *The Subtle Body: An Encyclopedia of Your Energetic Anatomy*. Sounds True Inc, 2009.

Dale, Cyndi. *The Complete Book of Chakra Healing* (2nd ed.). Llewellyn Publications, 2010.

Glasson, Natalie. *The Twelve Rays of Light*. Derwen Publishing, 2010.

Hovland, S. "Vibratory Grid Activation." 2000. Unpublished notebook.

Jacka, Judy. *The Vivaxis Connection: Healing Through Earth Energies*. Hampton Roads Publishing, 2000.

Kessler, Steven. *The 5 Personality Patterns; Your Guide to Understanding Yourself and Others and Developing Emotional Maturity*. Bodhi Tree Press, 2016.

McFetridge, Grant. *Peak States of Consciousness: Theory and Application*. Institute for the Study of Peak States Press, 2004.

Nienaber, Jeannette. *The Heart in You: A Personal Journey through Your Physical, Emotional, Mental and Spiritual Heart*. Balboa Press, 2019.

Noël, Rudy. *The Huggin' Healer*. Publish America, 2011.

Pierrakos, John. *Core Energetics*. LifeRhythm Publication, 1990.

About the Authors

After working together for several years, Tim McConville and Franny Harcey were Divinely guided to share their collective wisdom, and Awakening Healing Axis was born. Through the synergy of their collaboration, they have found it possible to go much deeper into the work of personal healing and supporting others in their quest for self-healing and transformation. With individual backgrounds in various energy modalities, Tim and Franny have created work that focuses on raising their collective frequency and those they share with, in order to contribute to the ascension of human consciousness.

This unique approach incorporates new healing techniques, increasing our understanding of the science supporting energy therapies while linking to the development of new insights among esoteric healing, human physiology, and energy therapy through the multi-dimensional bio fields. To learn more, please visit awakeninghealingaxis.com

Franny's Story

Growing up in Minnesota, my perfect day was being outside communing with nature. I also found great solace in going to church and connecting with God in the way I knew at that time. When I was really young, I saw myself being a nun one day. Later, I shifted to following my heart and connecting with the Divine through meditation and a deeper personal spiritual connection.

As a small child, I was quite aware of "seeing and sensing" the spirits around my parents' home. I remember them vividly, but when I reached the age of about seven or eight, they began to frighten me for some reason, so I adamantly tuned them out and shut off my ability to see and sense them. I don't recall my abilities returning until I was in my late 20s when I had my children.

My early career was as a hairstylist. Working on clients' hair and being in such close proximity to them was a difficult time for me, as I am strongly empathic and had little ability to discern what was mine and what was not at that time. I would experience physical sensations such as pain or emotional upset, including tears. I recall thinking I was a bit loopy and going crazy. In truth, I was in serious energetic overload.

In 2000, I was pointed to a Healing Touch class. The energy training was lifesaving as I finally began to realize my empathic nature and gifts. It took me a long time to discern what was mine and what was not and how to self-regulate and support my own energy instead of unconsciously taking on someone else's challenges.

Over the course of more than two decades, I have studied with great healers and feel very blessed to have been present with so many at the time that I was so that I could embrace many different ways of being, learning, and bringing forth healing work. Each added to my toolkit to support me in the continual opening to the gifts I have and why I am here on the earth at this time. Since then, I have had the honor of working with thousands of clients over the past 20 years.

One of my great passions is mentoring others in the healing arts. I am blessed to be able to mentor many energy workers that are exploring who they are and how to be the best that they can be, first for themselves and then for the family, friends, or clients they work with.

Tim's Story

I have spent much of my life as a seeker. I was raised Catholic, but by adolescence, I yearned for more than Catholic teachings were offering. During much of my adult life, I voraciously read about all things metaphysical. At some point, I realized that what I was looking for could not be found in a book. I also participated in meditation groups and dabbled in some healing work. I made a few spiritual trips to India, spending my time in ashrams and studying Vedic spirituality. I considered myself a closet mystic, as most of my time went to career and family. I didn't really dive deep into healing work until my 50th year.

My college training was in environmental engineering. Much of my career focused on applying computers and automation to environmental issues. As a manager and VP in a consulting engineering firm, I was reluctant to share my deeper interests publicly. My work world was full of scientific thinkers who tended to be skeptical about things that could not be measured. I, too, struggled internally as my engineering training taught me to trust the scientific process. It took a couple of firsthand experiences to convince my engineer brain that the energetic world is truly real.

For the last 20 years, my interests and priorities shifted to the healing arts and exploring the unseen world of the spiritual. I was formally trained in Healing Touch and then expanded into other modalities. 15 years ago, I retired early from the corporate world to devote my efforts to teaching and client work in the energy healing field. As my healing and teaching practice grew, so did my trust in the unseen guides that would show me different techniques to use for healing. Our current work is built on that deep trust and the ever-expanding possibilities that unfold as we deepen our understanding of our spiritual and energetic nature.

Apprentices and Contributors

We would like to honor the contributions of the apprentices that contributed to the making of these workshops. They have said yes to working with Spirit and assisting the entire collective to raise its frequency.

Barbara DeMers

Barbara owns and operates a hair salon where she offers integrative energy healing services in addition to her spirit-filled presence behind the salon chair. Barbara empowers her clients to realize their Divinity through aligning their energy system, allowing the innate shift for healing to occur. Her passion is creating an energetic environment for harmony and balance, thereupon revealing the Truth of who we are. She has studied many healing modalities and is an ordained minister. Barbara has been expanding with Awakening Healing Axis since the first retreat and eagerly stepped into the role of AHA facilitator.

Sylvie Francoeur

Sylvie is a proud Healing Touch Certified Practitioner and has been trained in several other healing modalities. She is also an instructor of the HT for Children program. Sylvie is a certified trainer with the Canadian Mental Health Commission and has over 25 years' experience as a facilitator, helping organizations navigate change. She has deepened her personal spiritual journey since connecting with Awakening Healing Axis in 2018. She is thrilled by the love and light being brought forward by the AHA team and is humbled to be able to share this work, as a contributor, with an ever-growing number of people.

Perry Harcey

As a child, Perry was sensitive to universal energies and had an innate knowing of information. He would use his hands and focused thoughts to heal his own physical wounds. Being mechanically-inclined and process-oriented, Perry used his gifts in an aviation maintenance career as a technician, inspector, and manager. Many times, Perry found himself using his energetic awareness to connect with the aircraft and receive information on what it needed, which helped to troubleshoot, repair, and maintain the aircraft.

Within Awakening Healing Axis, Perry applies his gifts and knowledge to provide business and technical support services. He supports the energetic structure of AHA and receives and shares guided information for the support of the AHA community. With excitement and gratitude, he holds an integral part of AHA. Perry is committed to assist in bringing forward this body of work to support energetic and physical healing and to support the ascension of the collective human consciousness.

Michele Jahnke

Michele has a degree in business and brings her strength of operating a family business for 19 years to AHA. She is a Healing Touch Practitioner and has deep interest in spirituality, energetic, and sound healing for humans and animals. Michele's personal journey has inspired her to facilitate others in their own amazing journey of healing as she holds a deep presence for another on their path. She has graciously shared her wisdom and presence with AHA.

Joanne Kaufman

Joanne has been a Nationally Certified Massage Therapist since 2001 with an Associates in Occupational Studies (AOS) from Boulder College of Massage Therapy. She has studied, practiced, and received life-changing energy medicine work in numerous modalities. She integrates other energetic modalities and AHA's powerful energetic foundations and techniques into her massage therapy work. Joanne spent formative years in her 20s doing faith-based nonviolence work in conflict zones. In this work, she noticed how simple presence and deep listening allowed local partners to create new possibilities in their personal and communities' lives. This foundation underlies her particular passion for empowering each person to own, embrace, and follow their own healing paths and talents in their own timing. This commitment to deep listening to support each being's song has surfaced an affinity with crystals, as well as participating in the healing of Earth/Gaia. Joanne is so delighted and honored to be an AHA facilitator.

Jon Skedsvold

It was during Jon's deployments to Iraq (2003) and Kosovo (2009) that he started becoming keenly aware of the abundance of human suffering. This created in him the yearning to ask the deeper questions in life. "Who am I?" and "Why am I here?" The curiosity he had as a child came flowing forward as he began to contemplate these questions. As it turns out, asking those questions led him on an inner quest that he could not have imagined. Reading any book and talking to any person that seemed to lead him closer to the answers, he soon realized that the answers could only come from within! True knowing would come with personal deep healing. Delving into various healing modalities from others to support his personal healing proved invaluable. In 2019 Jon began studying Healing Touch, completing the first 3 Levels of Healing Touch Program curriculum. In October of 2020 he attended his first Awakening Healing Axis workshop. AHA created a deeper level of healing through these retreats and the incredible frequencies being introduced. It is with great excitement that Jon brings the wisdom he is guided to bring forward and to be a part of the AHA team and community. "I am humbled to have an opportunity to support this incredible work in the world."

Other Work by
Awakening Healing Axis

Everything is Energy (including you!)

Awakening to Higher Frequencies:
A Guidebook

Embodying Higher Frequencies:
A Guidebook to Accelerating Personal and Planetary Consciousness

Todo es energía (¡incluso tú!)

———

AHA offers web-based training to deepen the experience of the energies described in this book. These are useful tools for both those who are interested in self-development as well as the practicing energy practitioner. Our experience suggests that more frequent practice helps to entrain your energetic system to the higher frequencies, allowing one to experience these elevated states for longer and more frequently, thereby changing your experience in the world. Links to all AHA trainings are available on our website.

To learn more about AHA's work, including upcoming
books, workshops, and retreats, please visit:

www.AwakeningHealingAxis.com